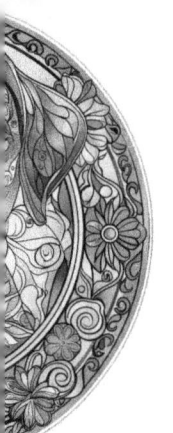 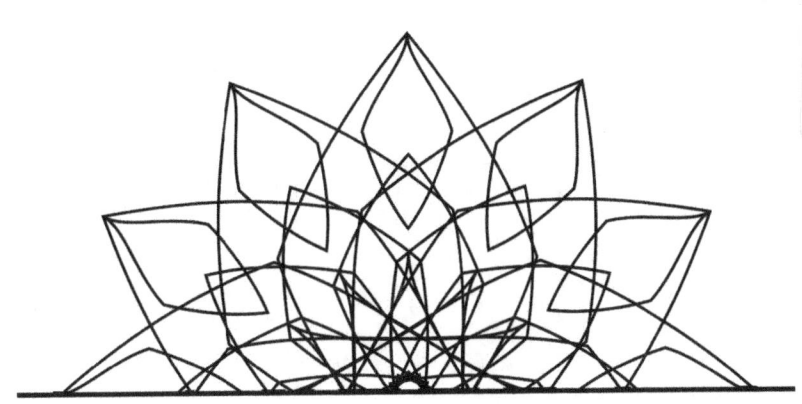 

Welcome to the enchanting world of Labrador mandalas!

Get ready to embark on a therapeutic journey filled with intricate designs inspired by the grace and charm of Labrador Retrievers. This coloring book is a celebration of the special bond between humans and these beloved canine companions. Whether you're a seasoned artist or new to the world of coloring, this book offers a creative outlet for all ages. Take a moment to unwind, destress, and reconnect with the soothing energy of Labrador Retrievers. So grab your favorite coloring tools, find a cozy spot, and let your creativity flow as you bring these Labrador mandalas to life. Thank you for joining us on this colorful adventure!

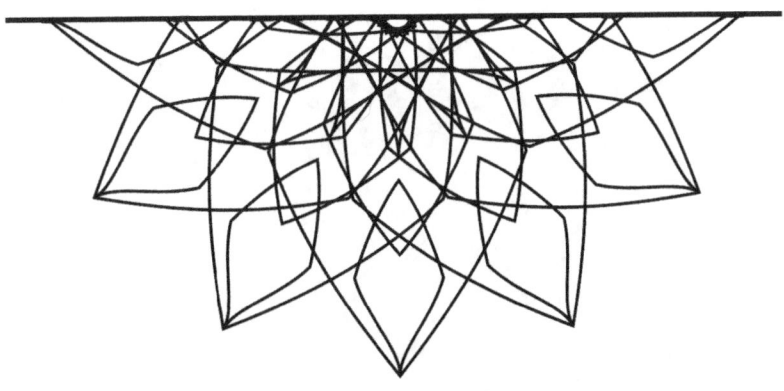

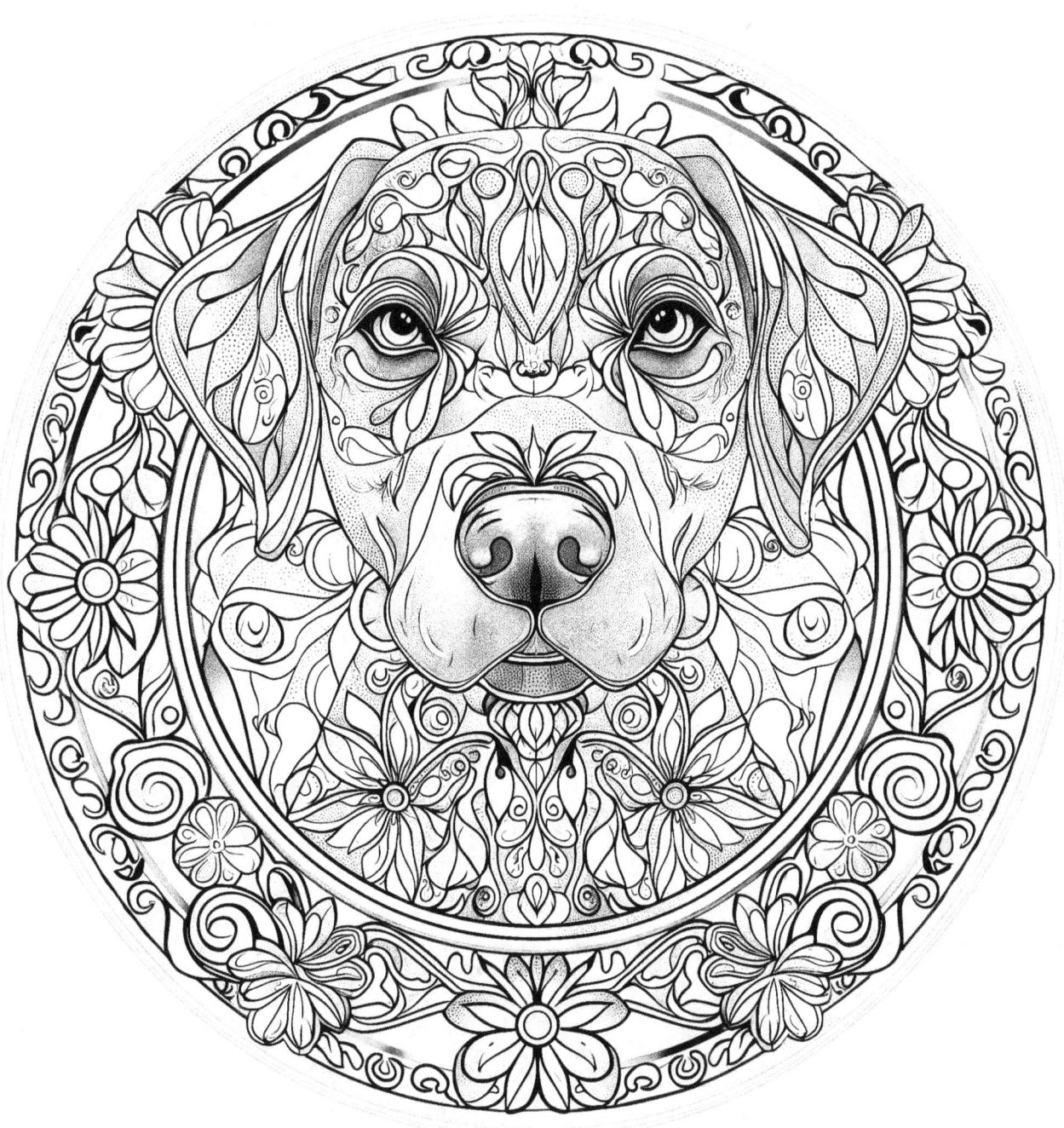

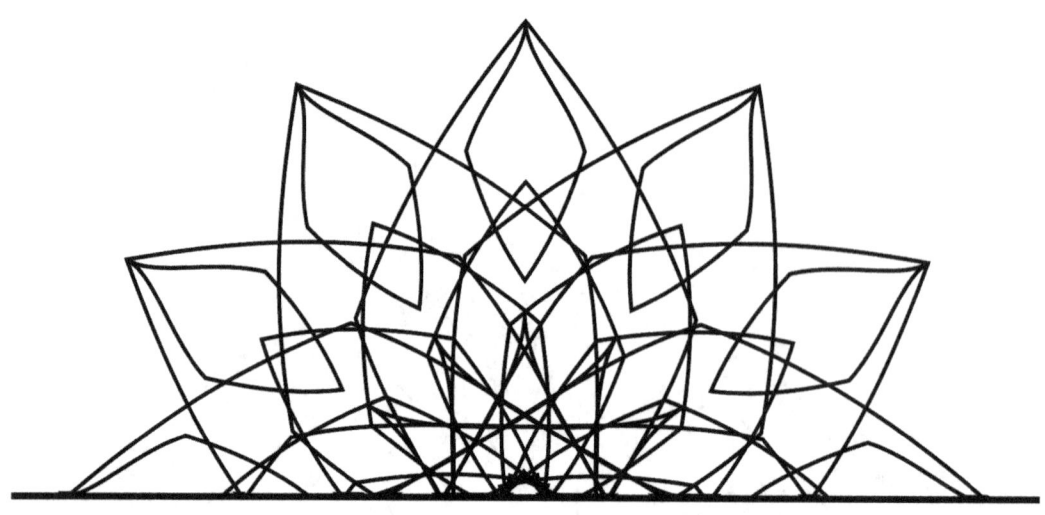

Labradors are originally from Newfoundland, Canada.

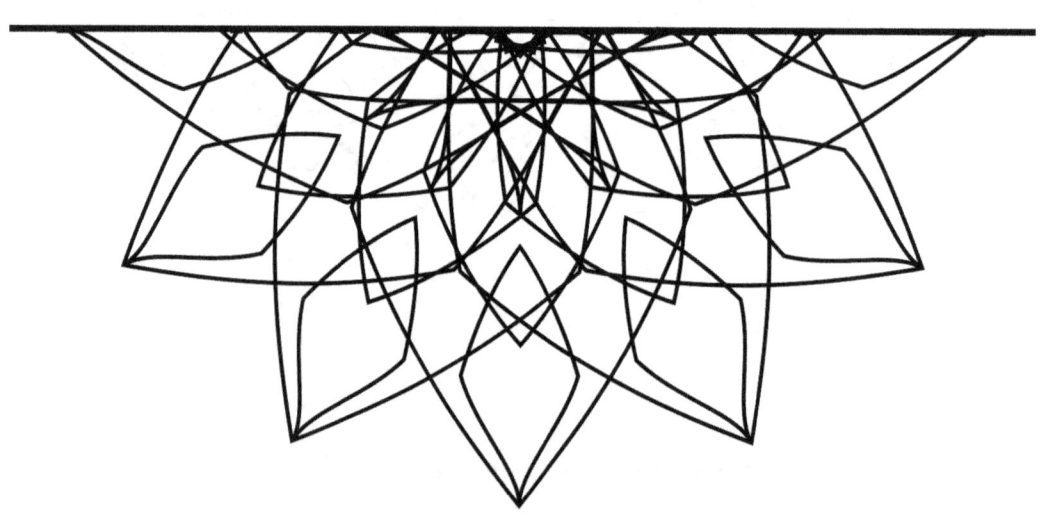

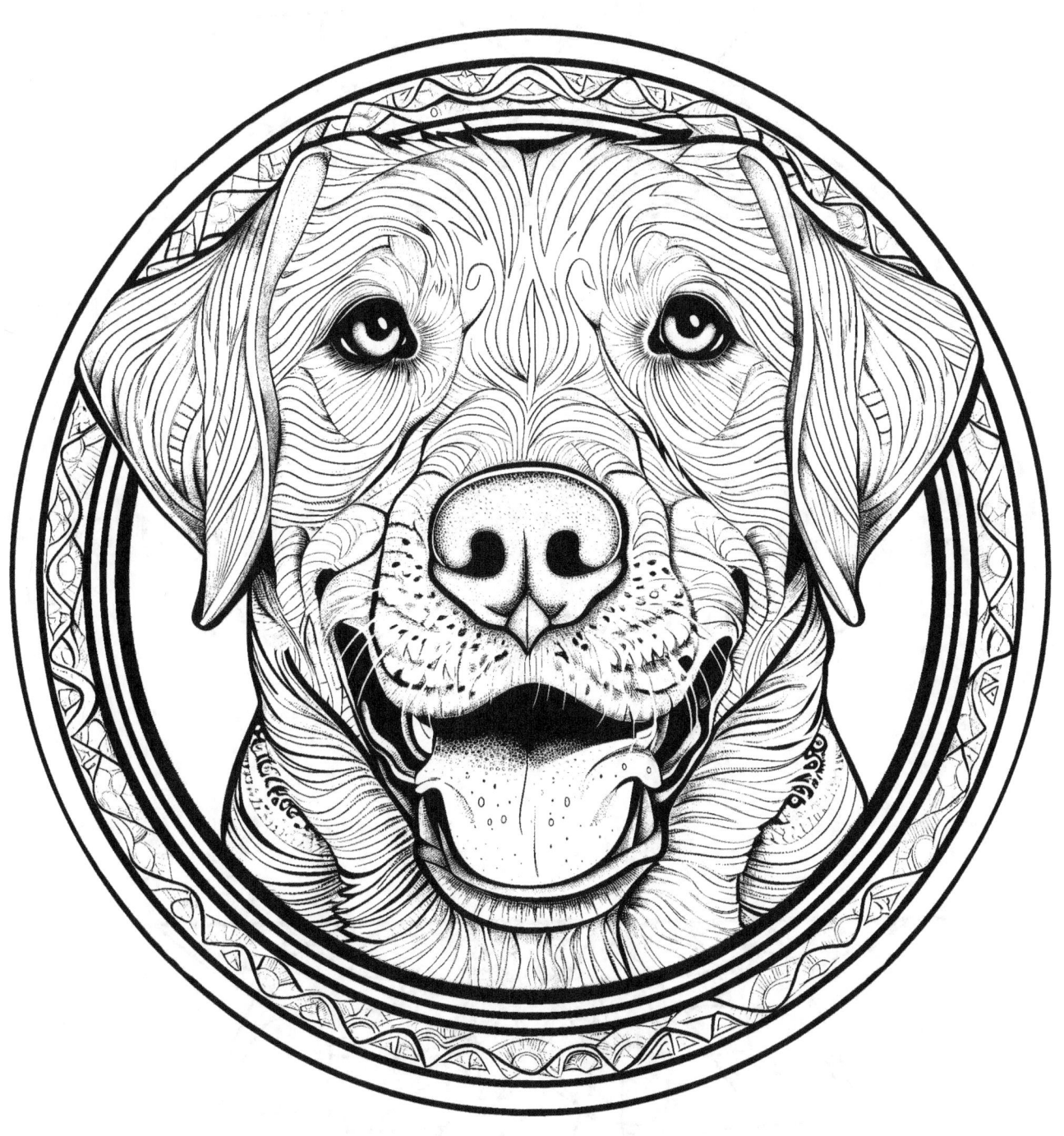

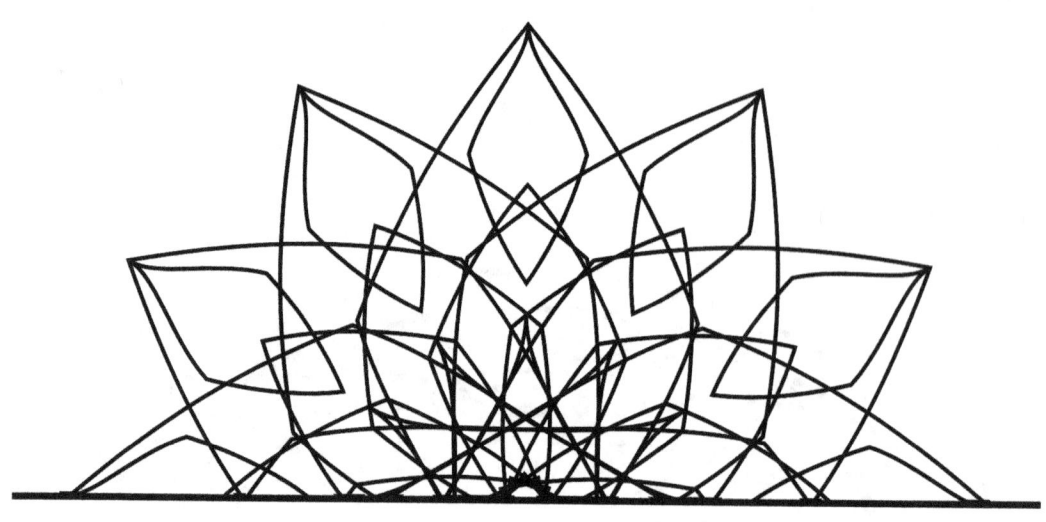

They are one of the most popular dog breeds worldwide.

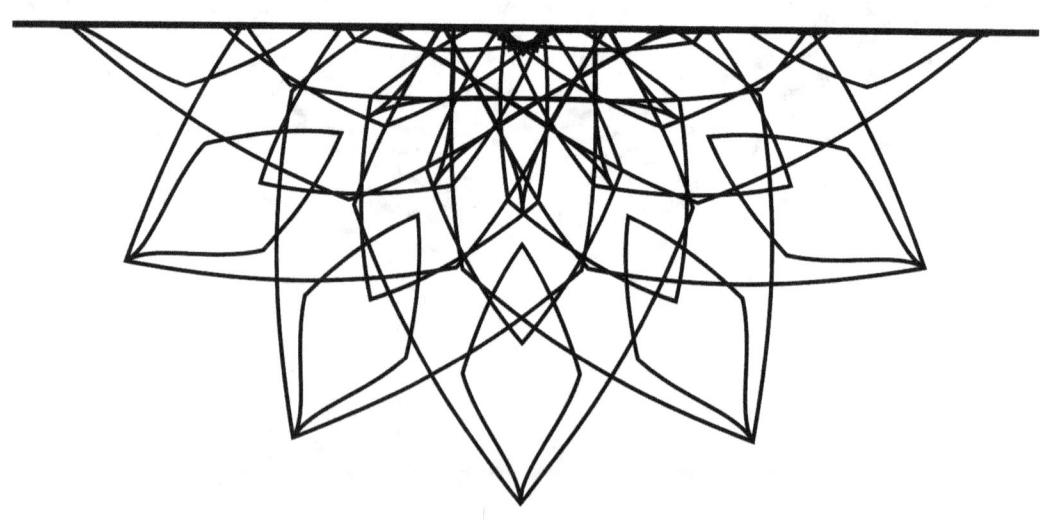

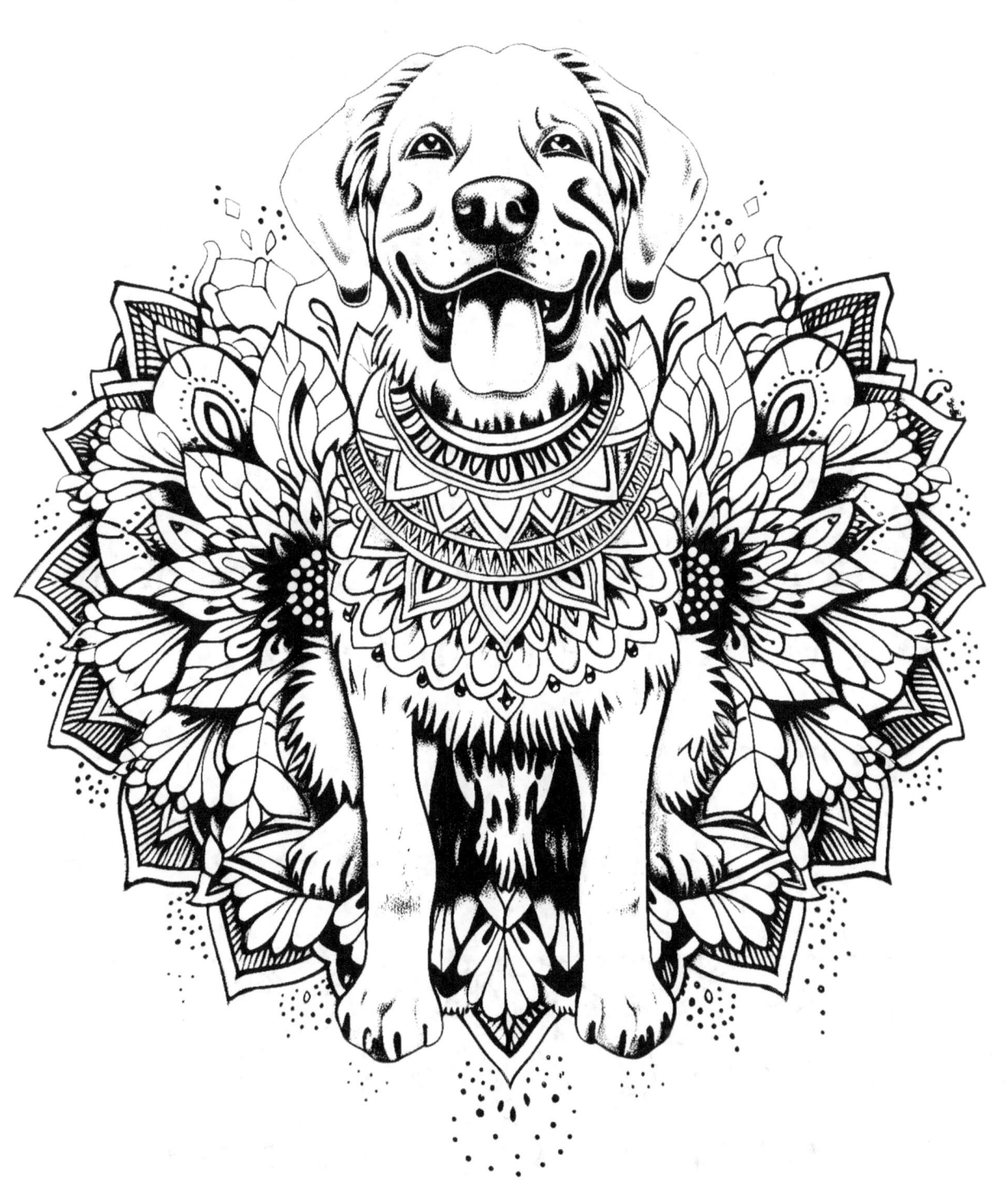

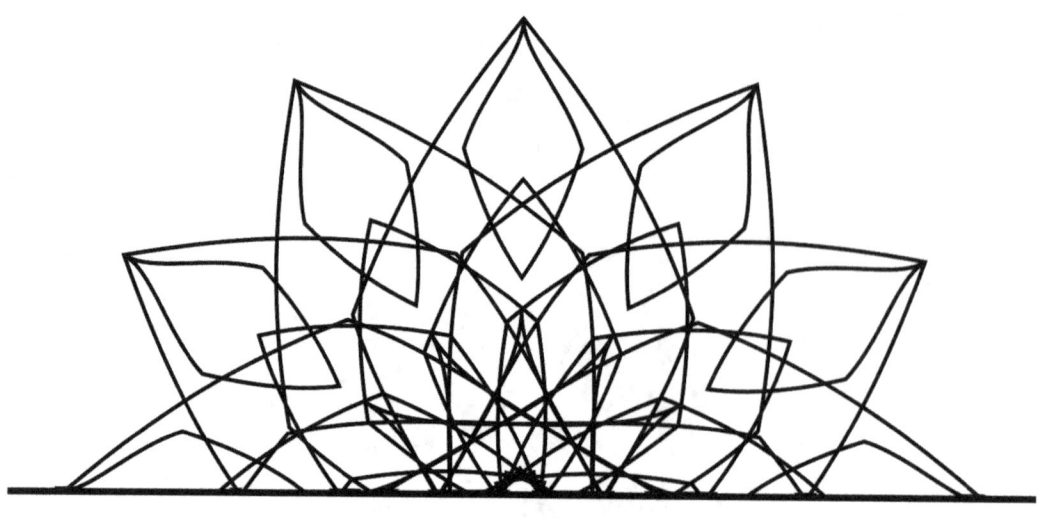

Labradors are known for their friendliness and gentle nature.

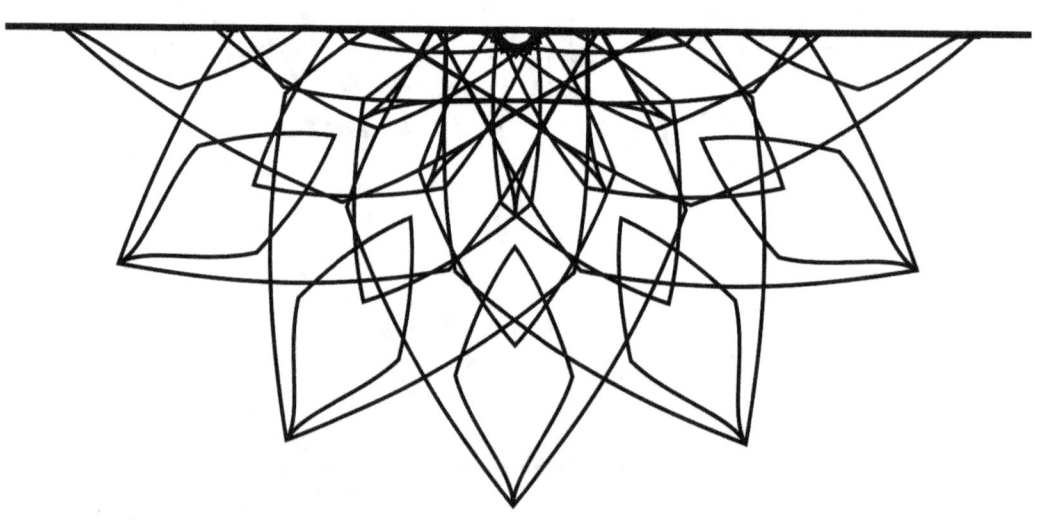

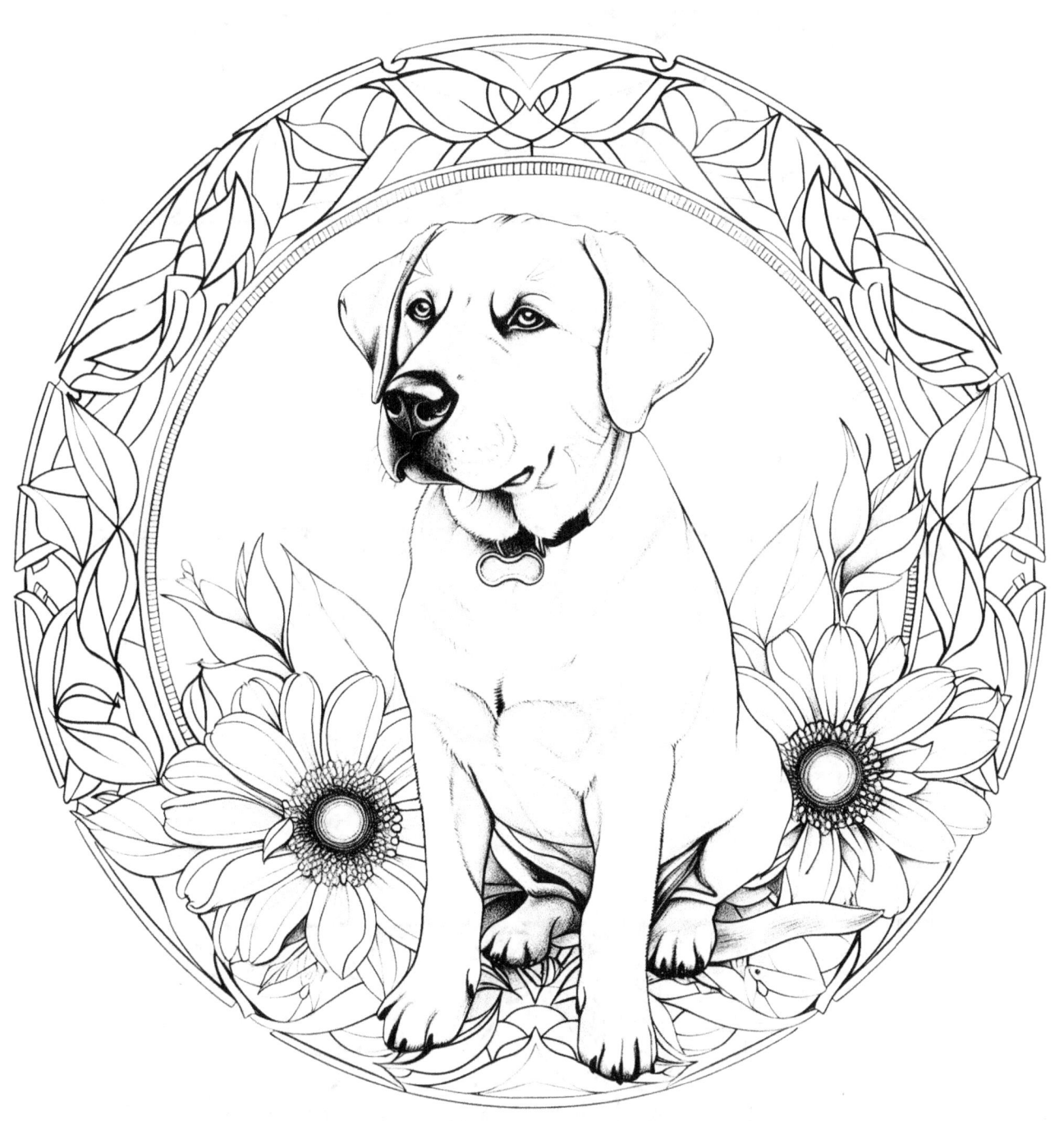

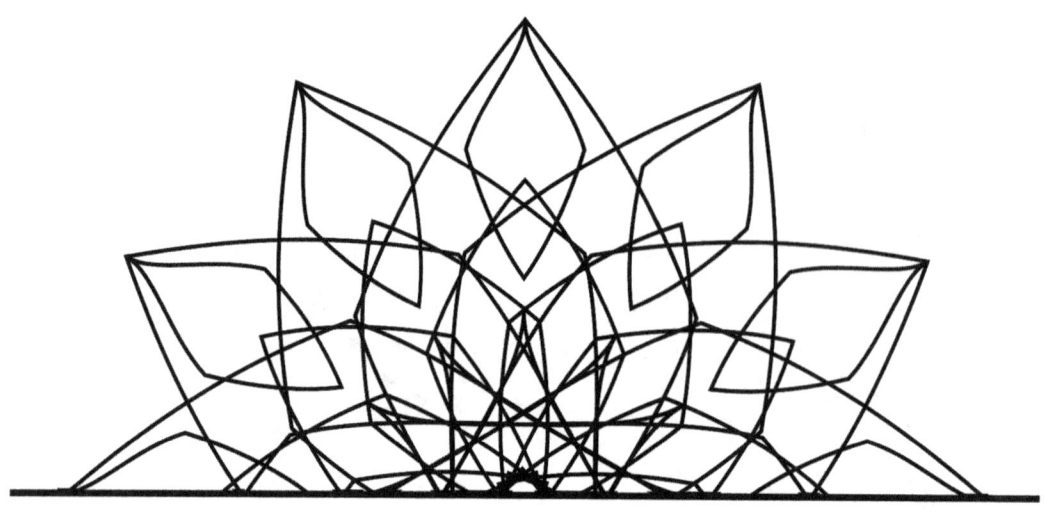

They originated as hunting dogs to assist in duck hunting.

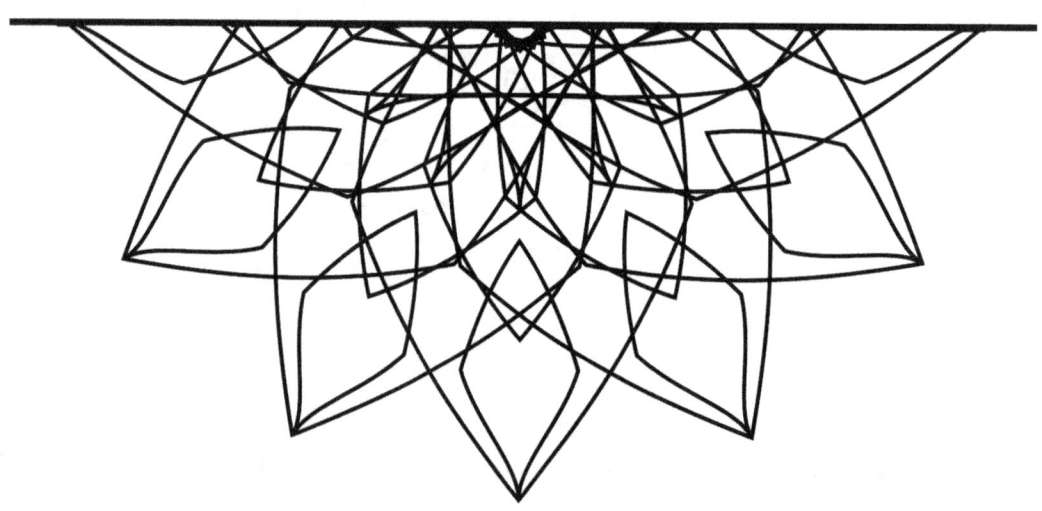

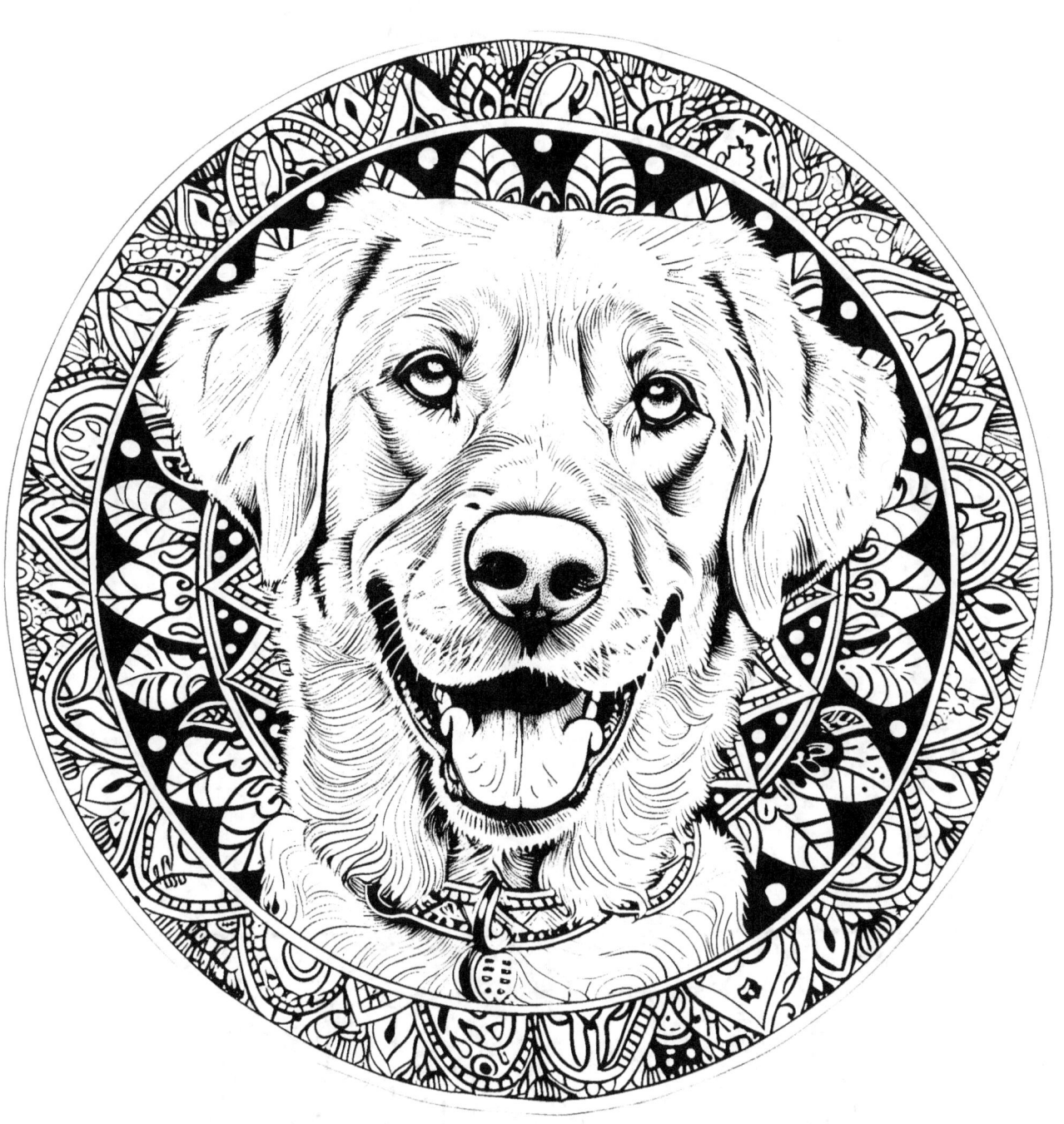

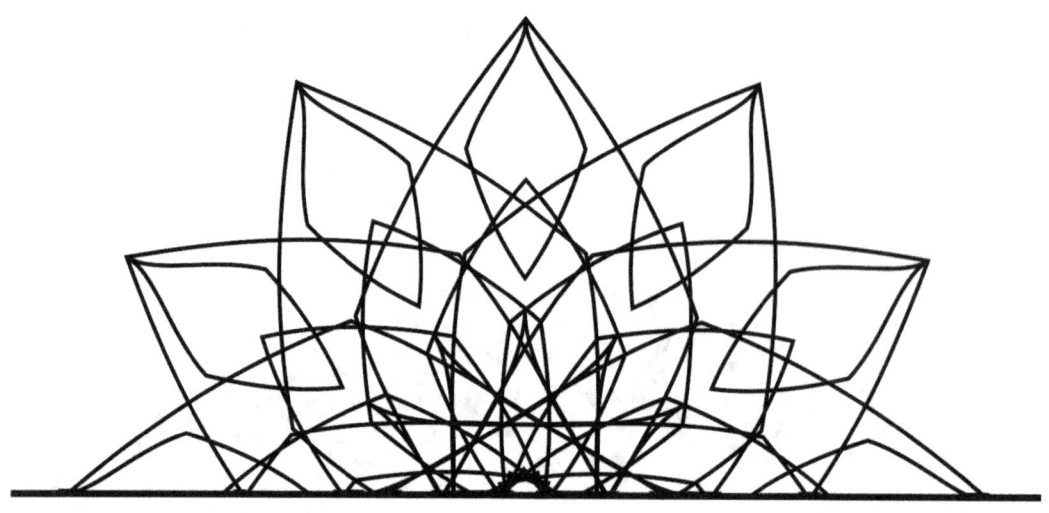

Labradors have water-repellent fur and love to swim.

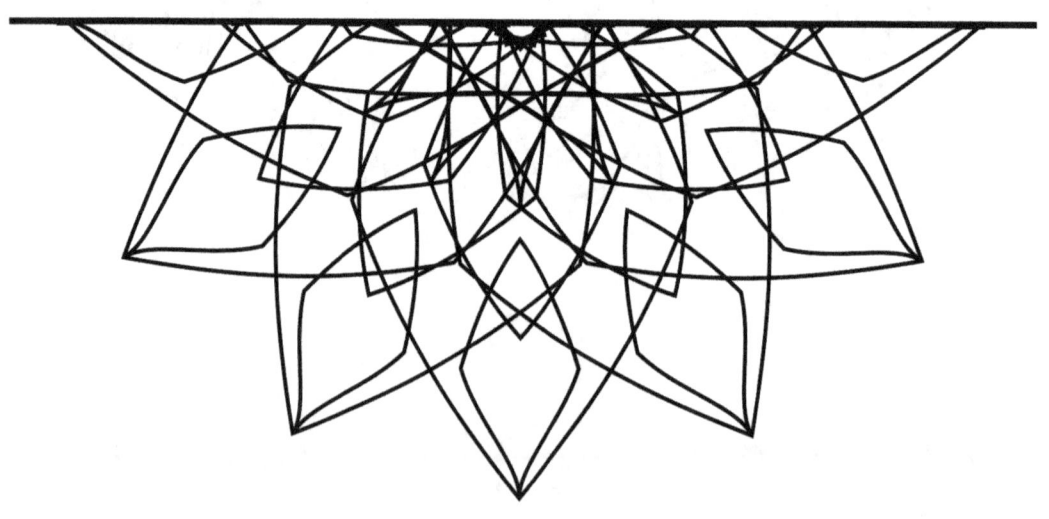

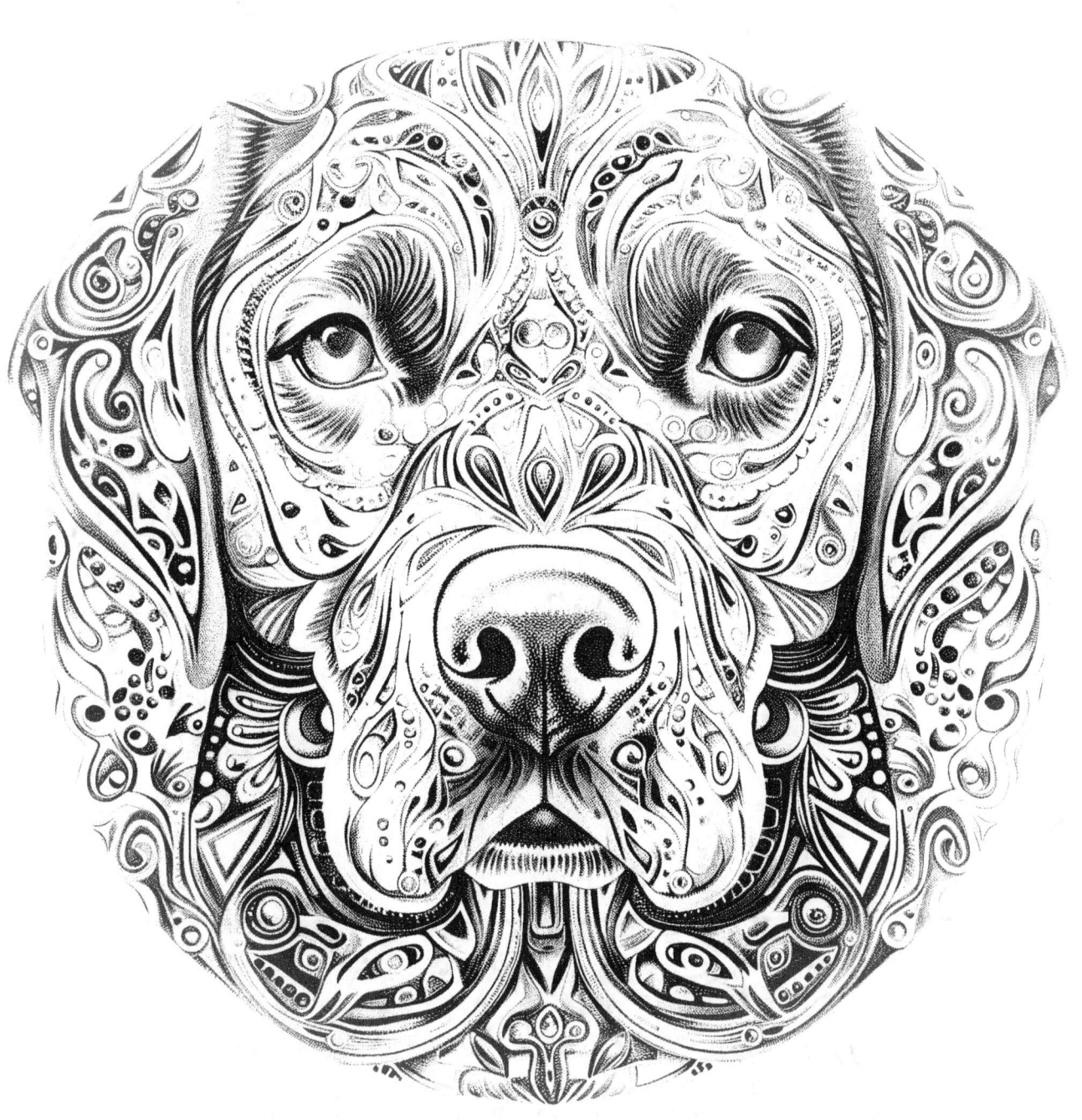

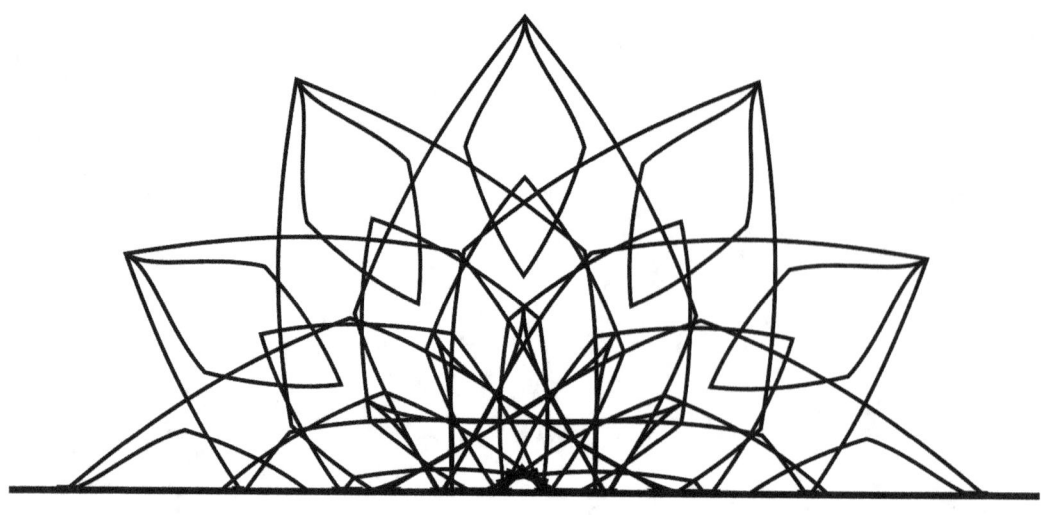

Their fur colors can be black, yellow or brown.

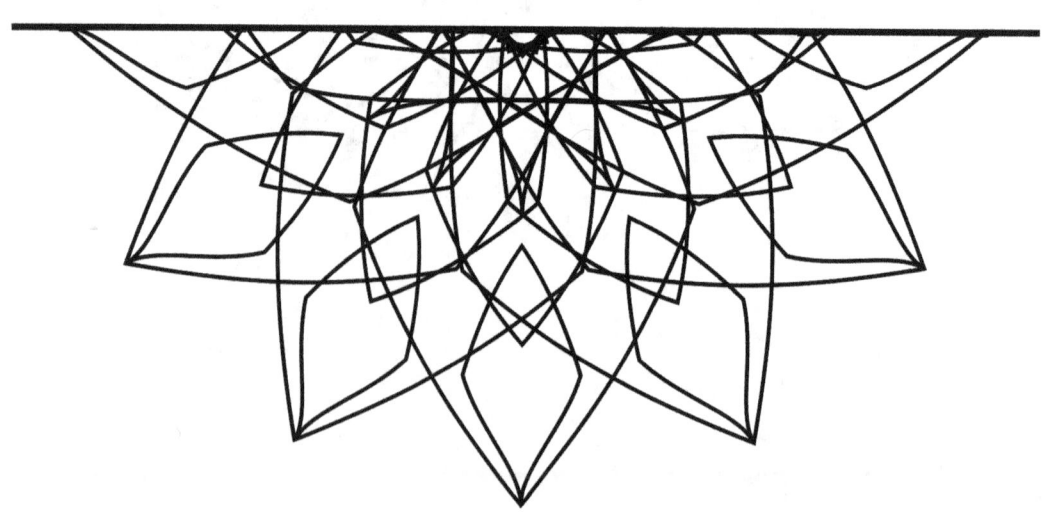

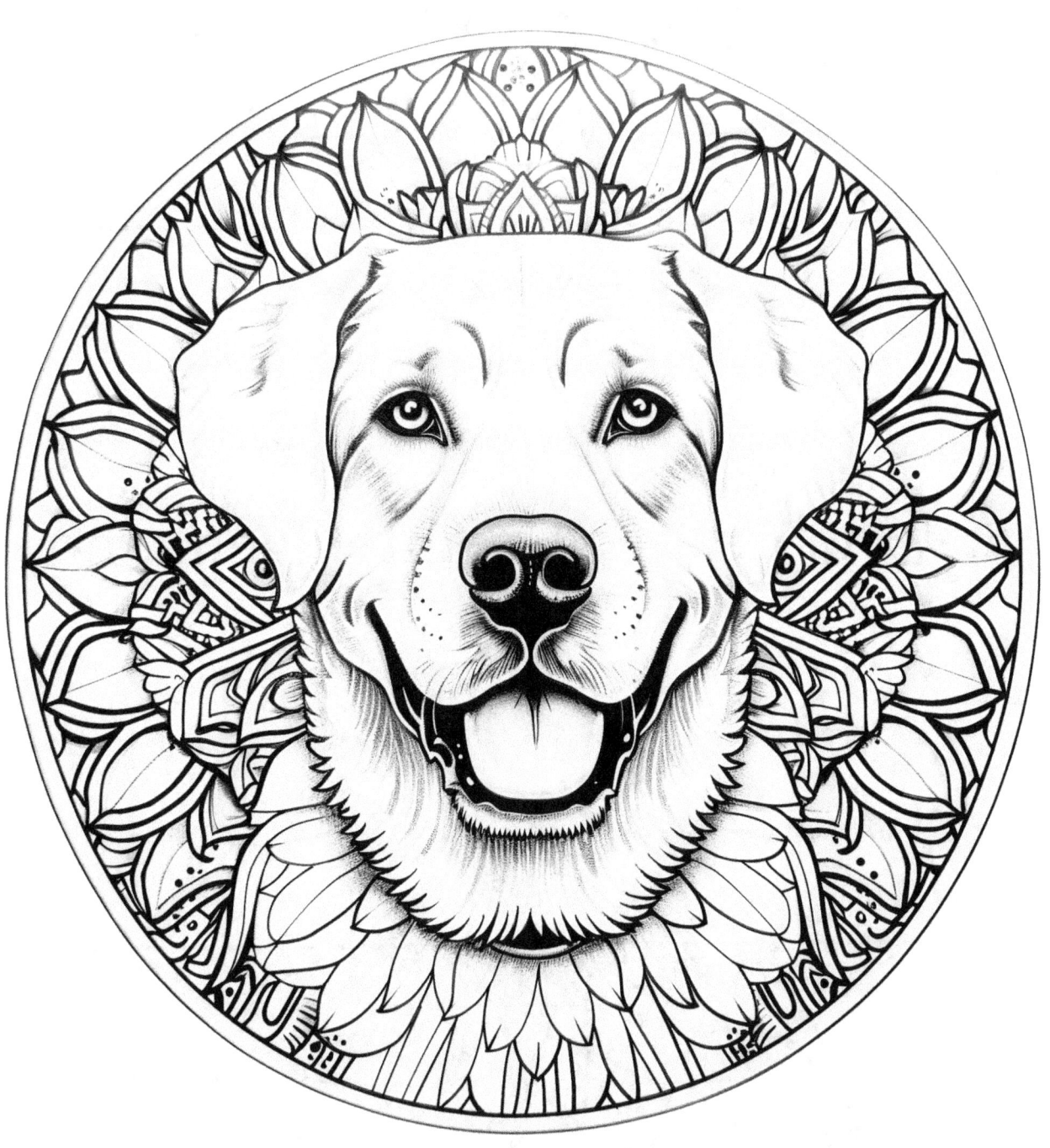

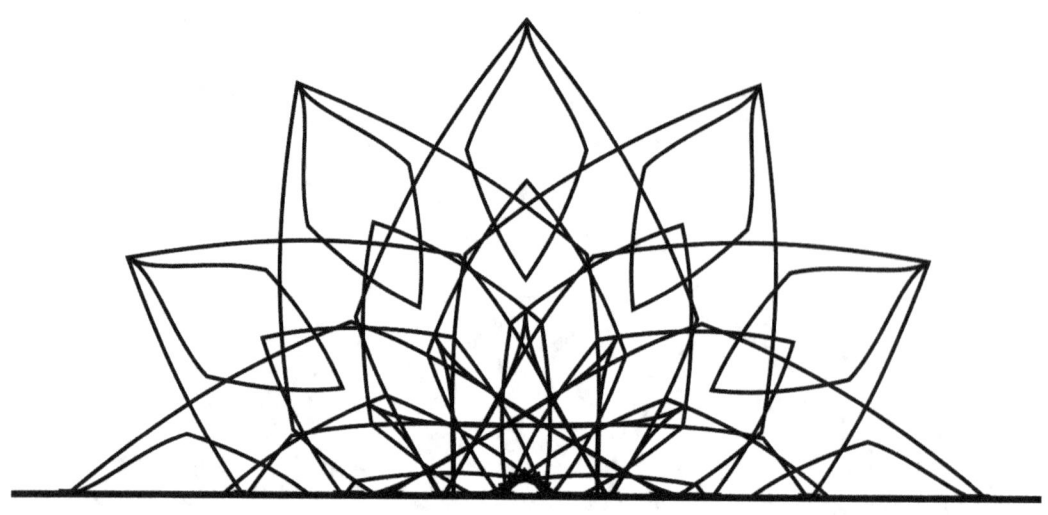

Labradors are very intelligent and easy to train.

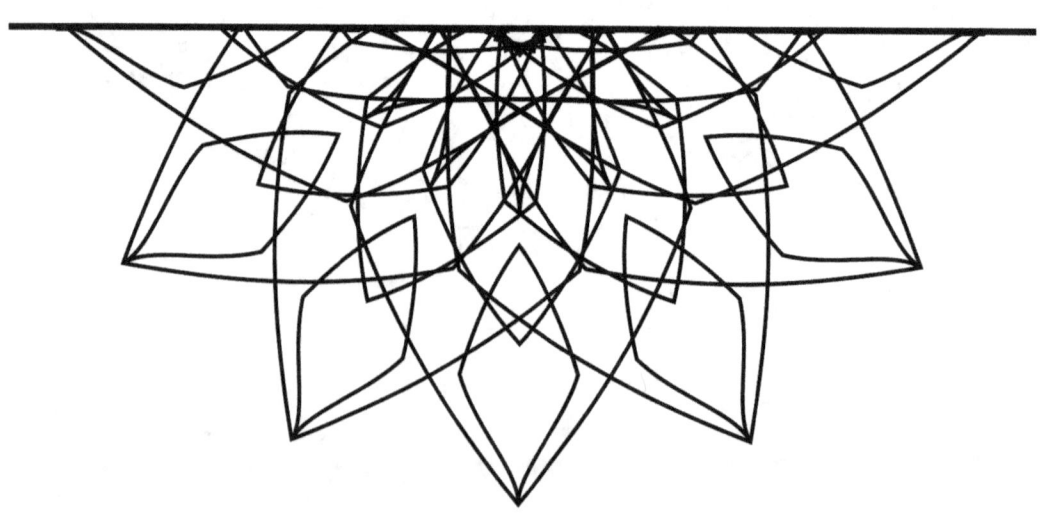

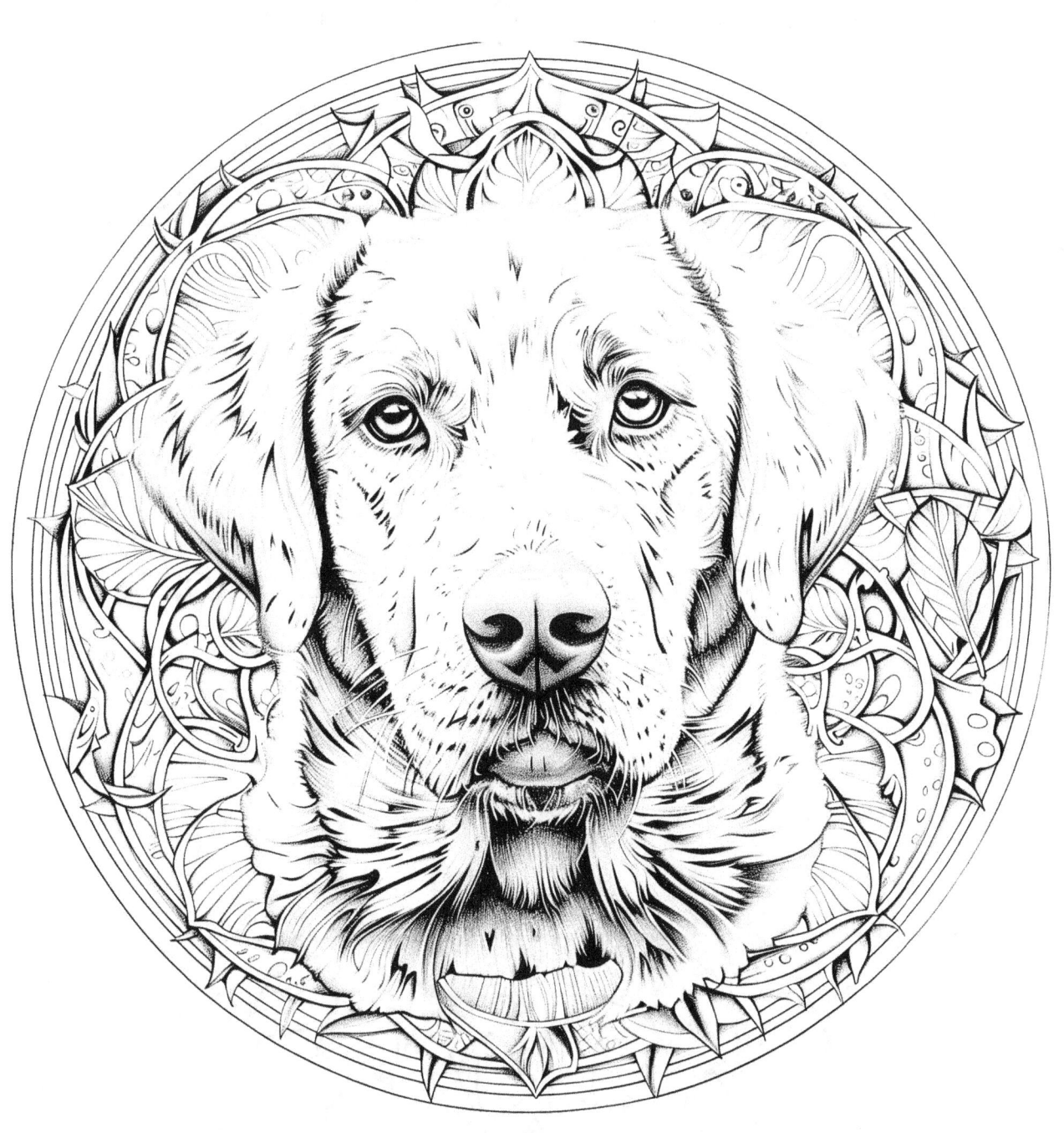

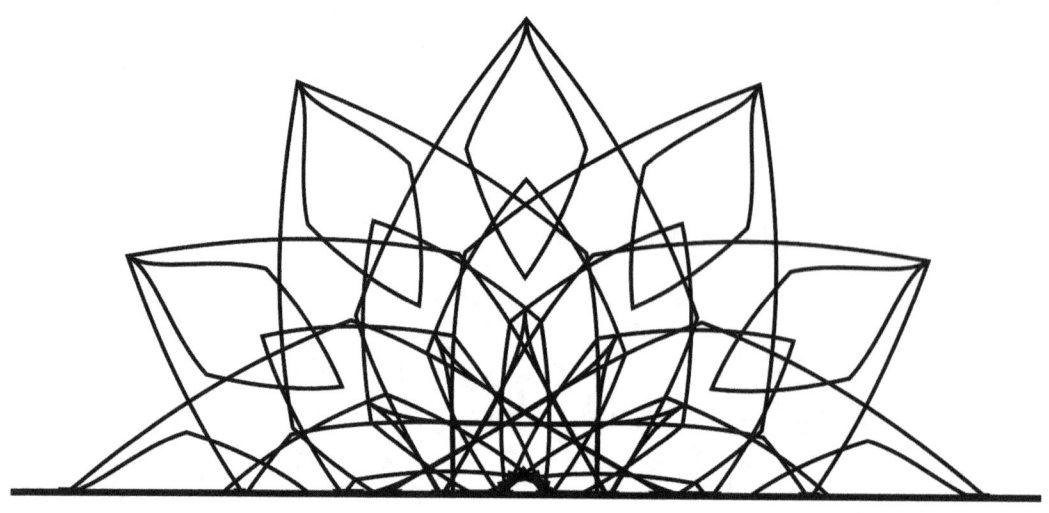

They are known for their excellent noses
and are often used as sniffer dogs.

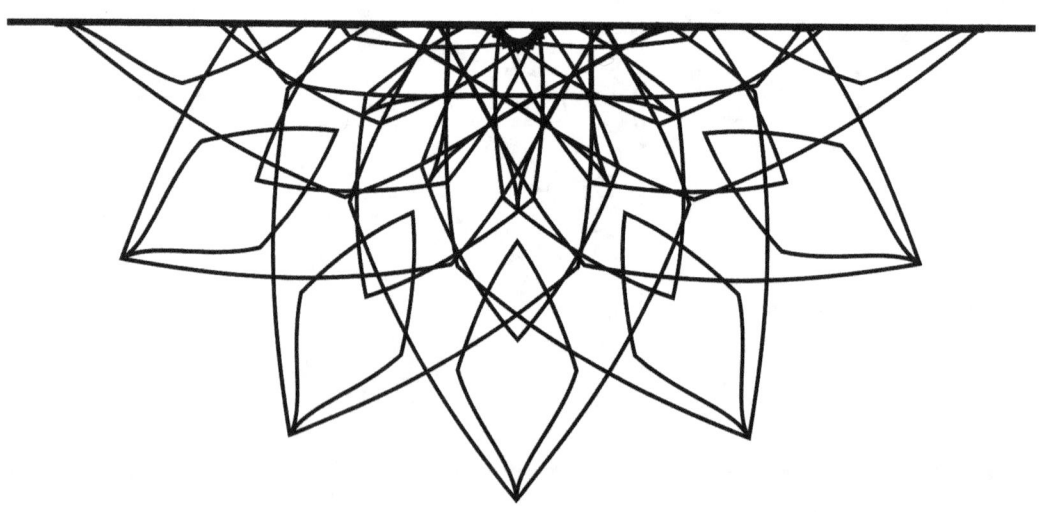

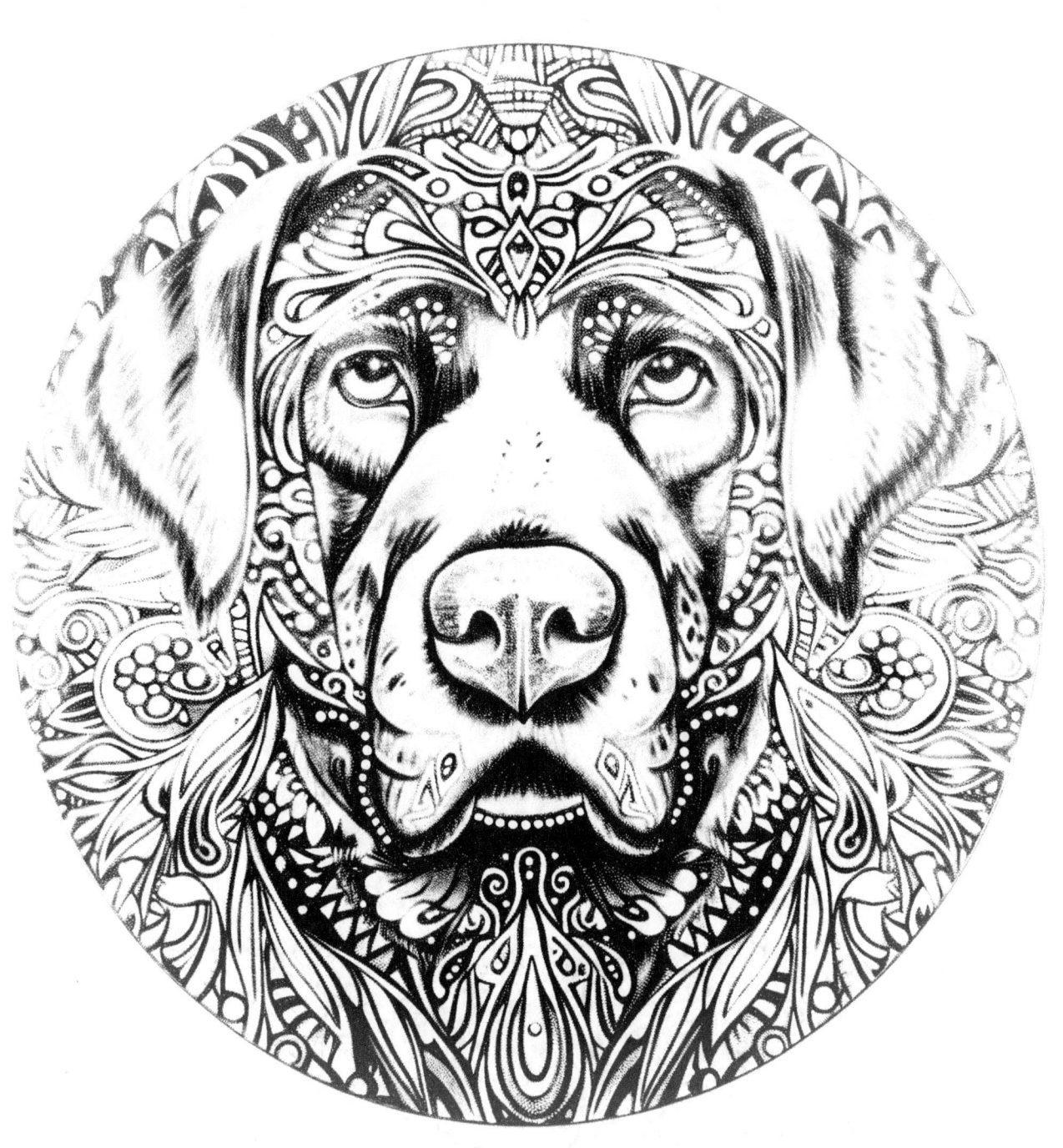

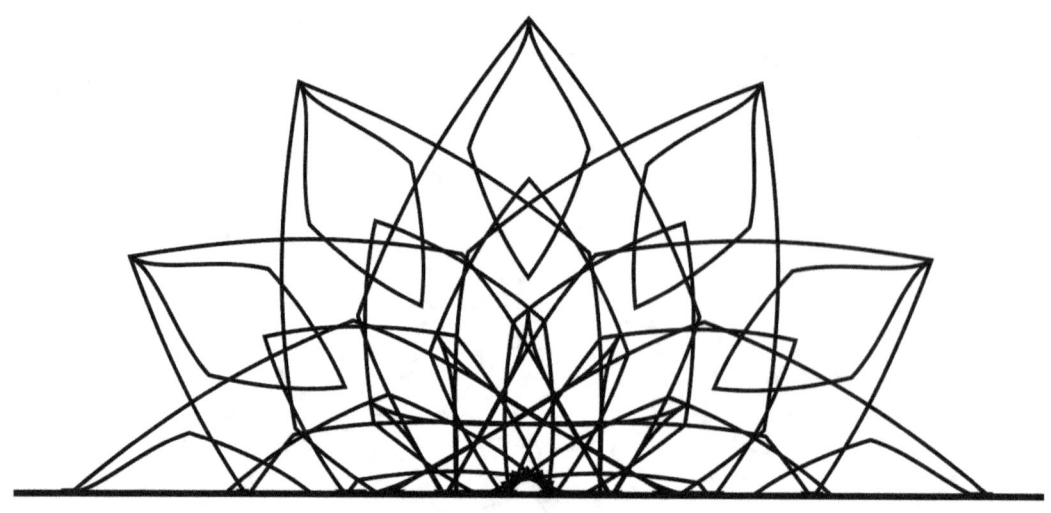

Labradors have a strong appetite and tend to eat anything they can find.

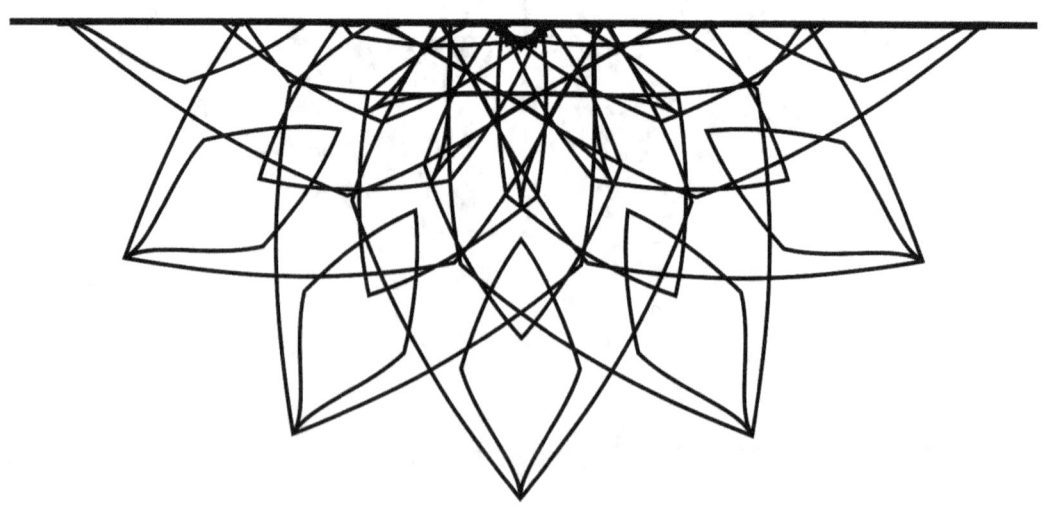

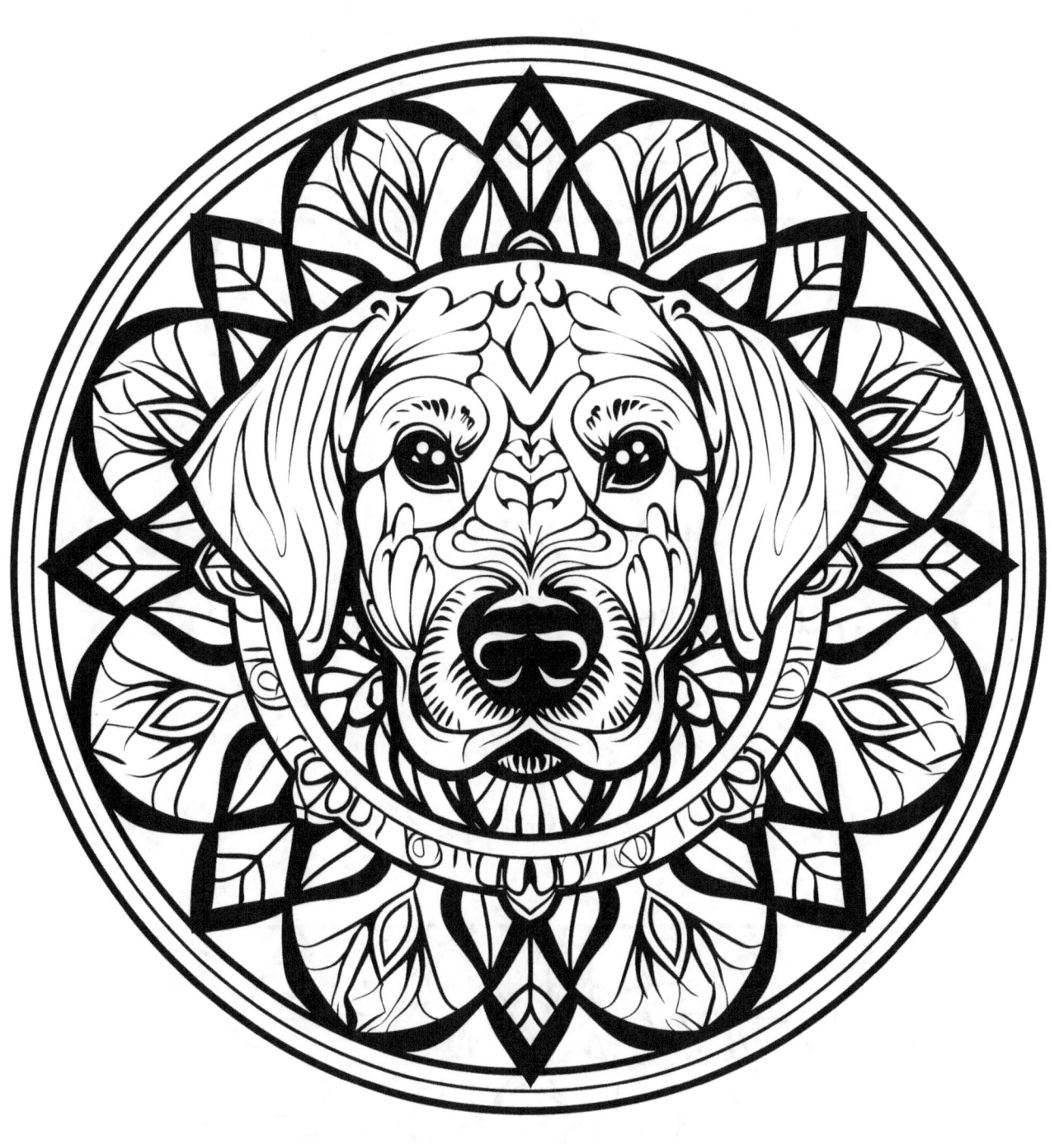

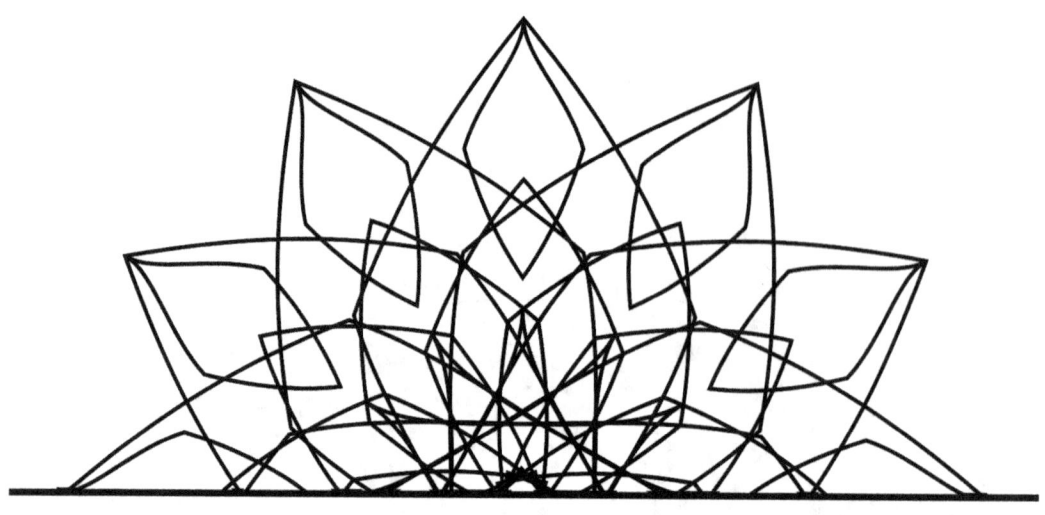

They are also very popular as family dogs and are good with children.

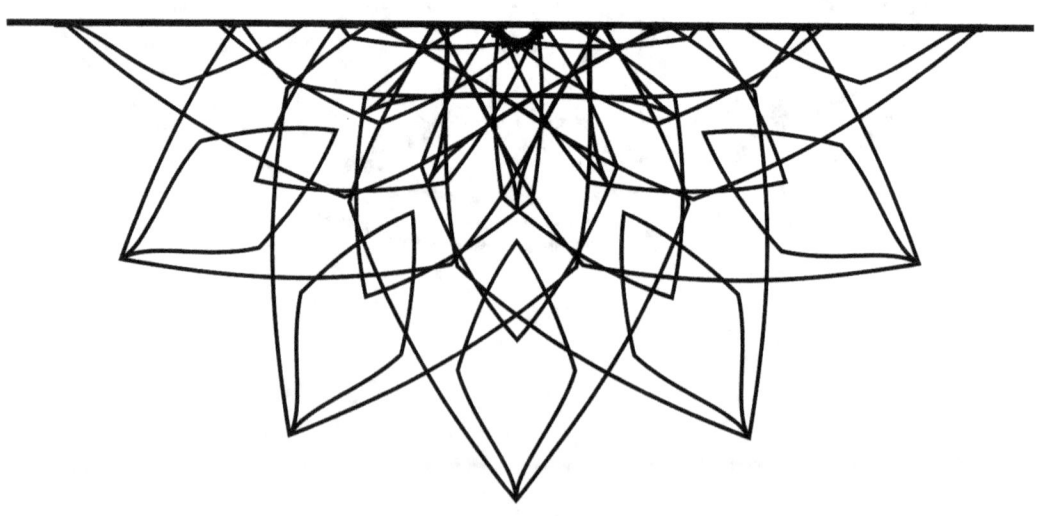

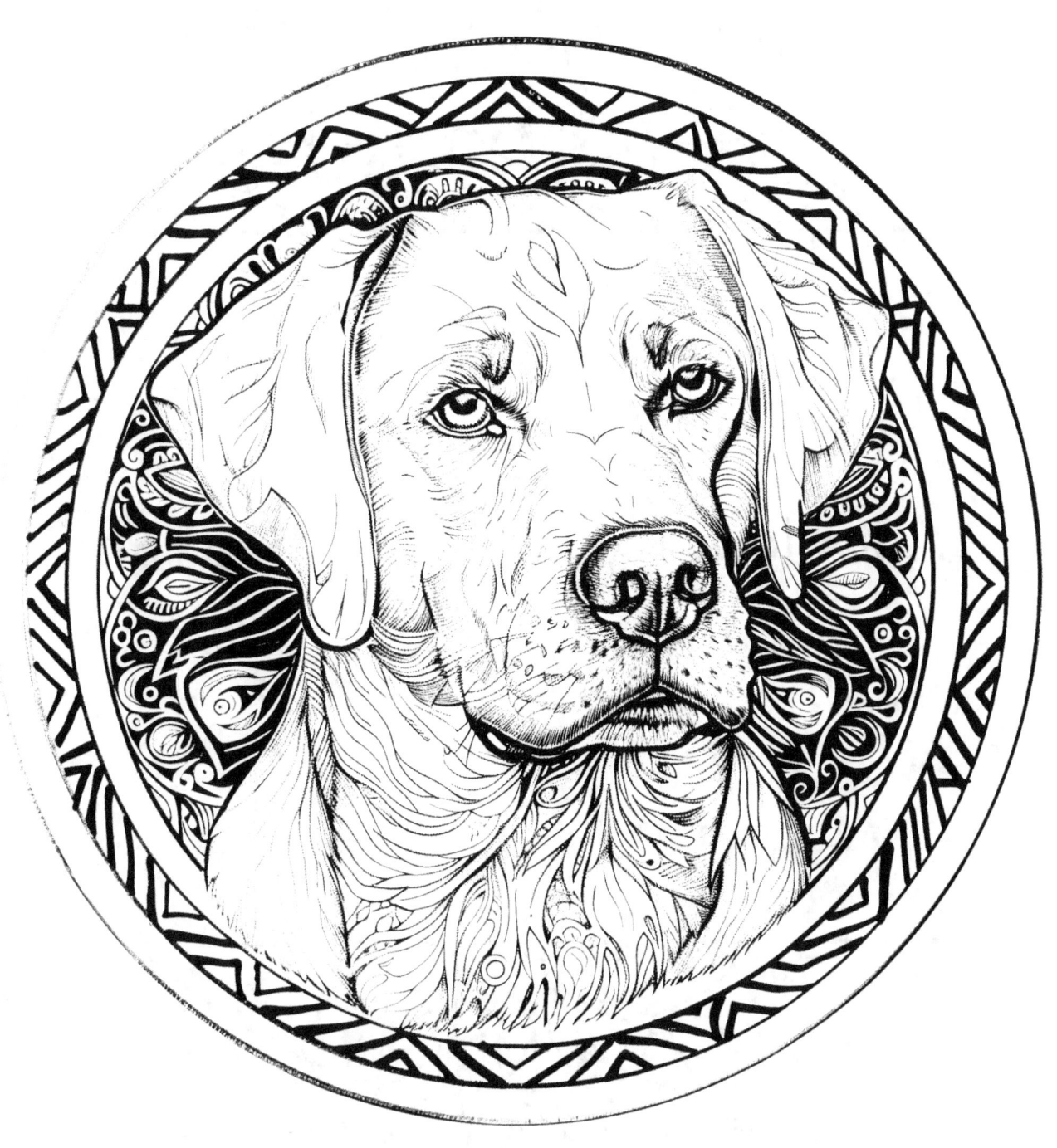

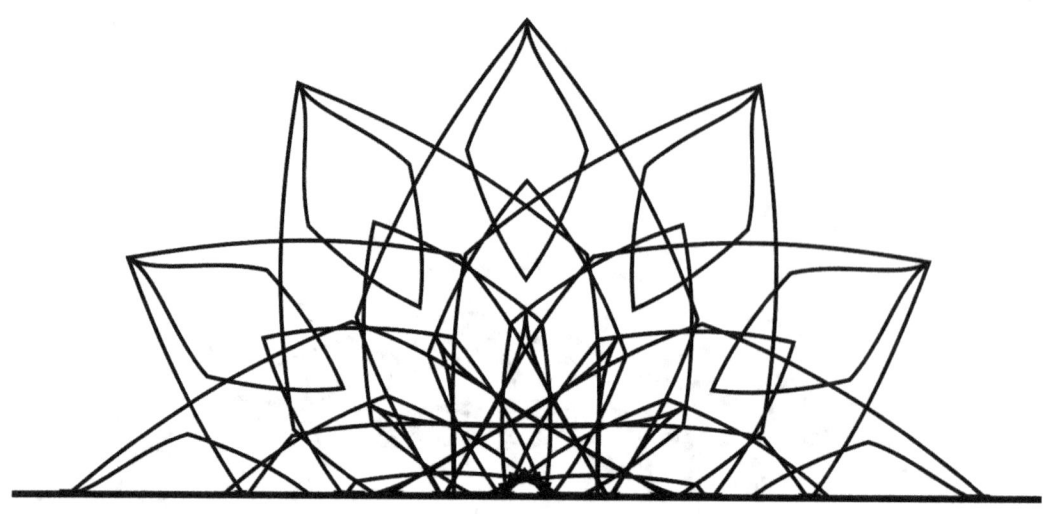

Labradors are energetic dogs and require a lot of exercise.

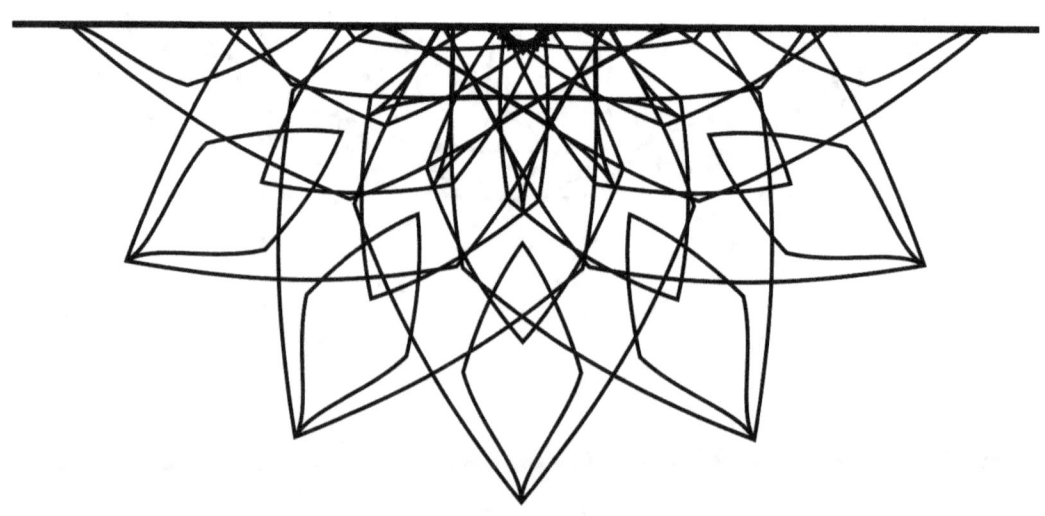

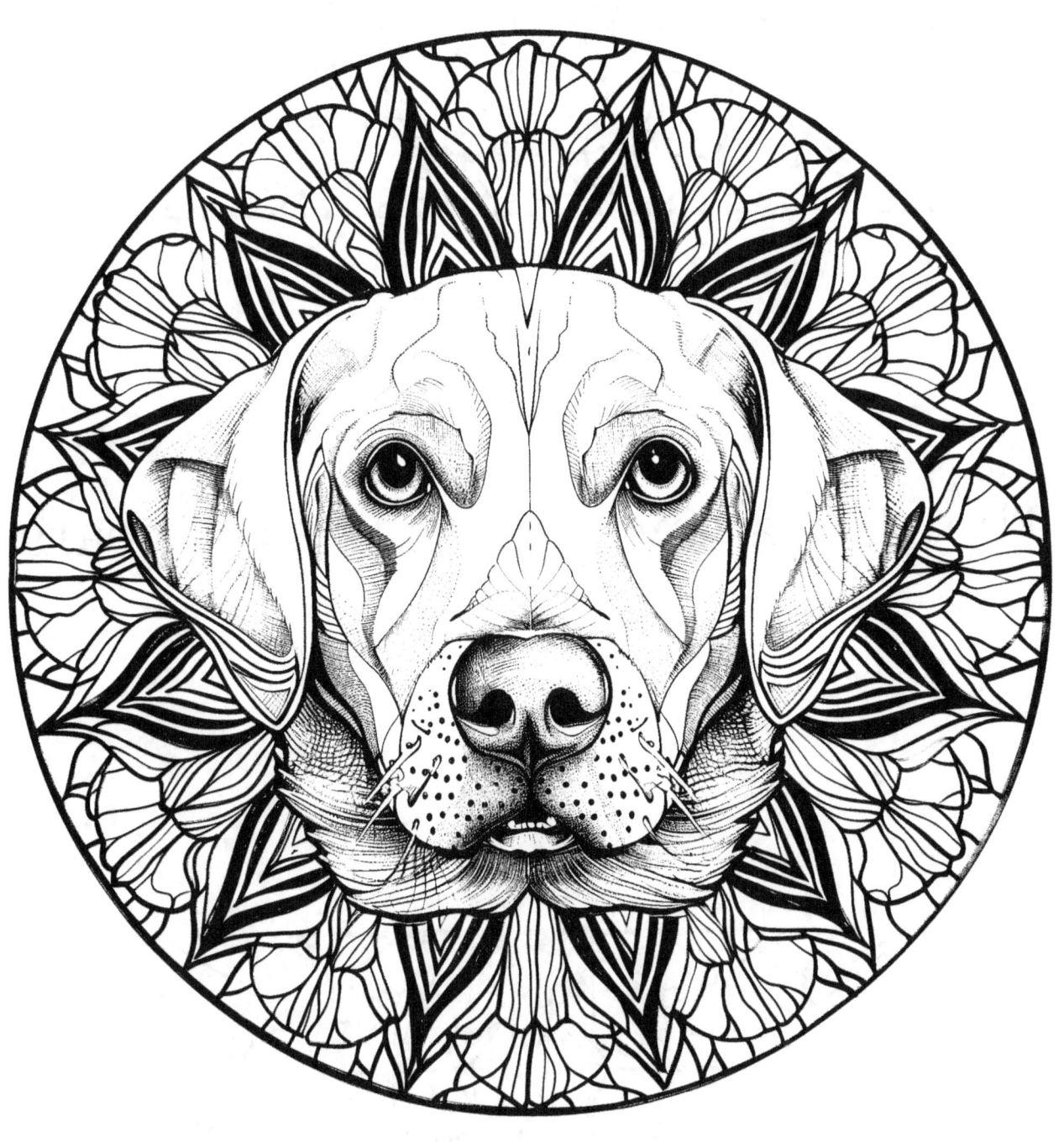

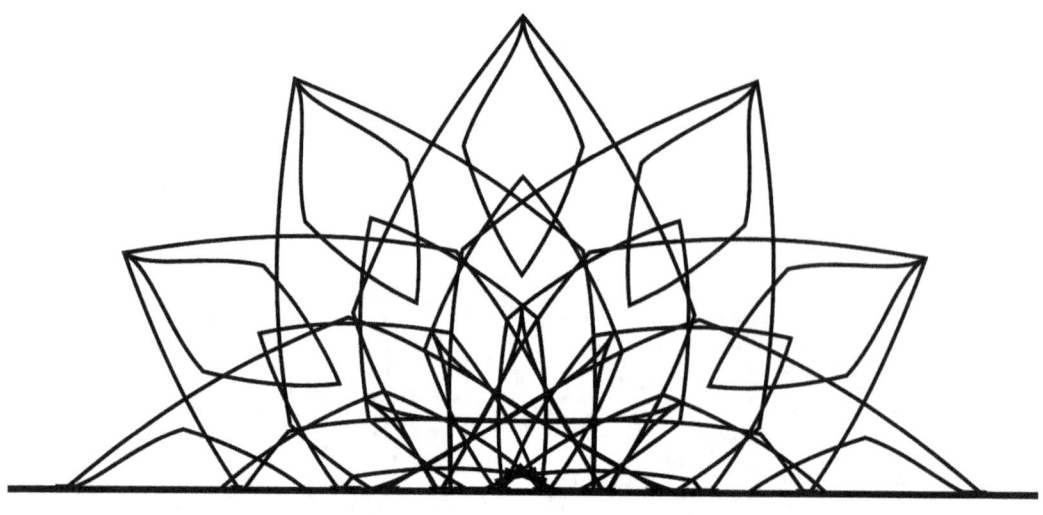

They live an average of 10 to 12 years.

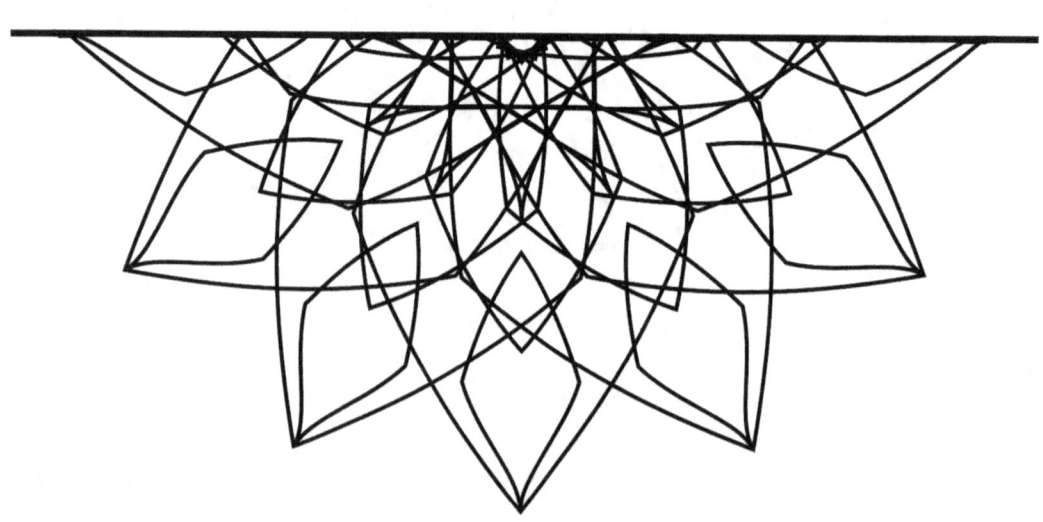

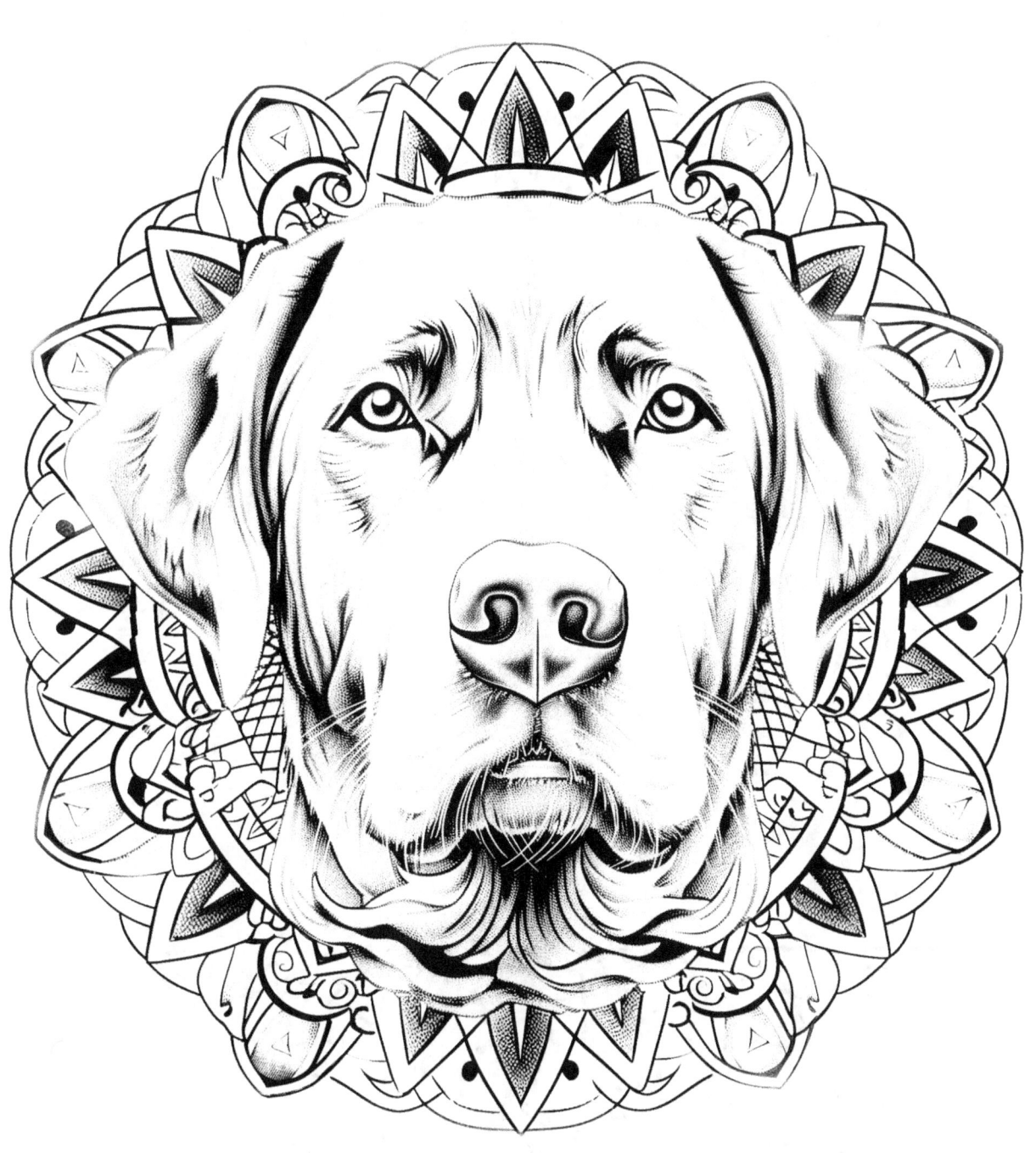

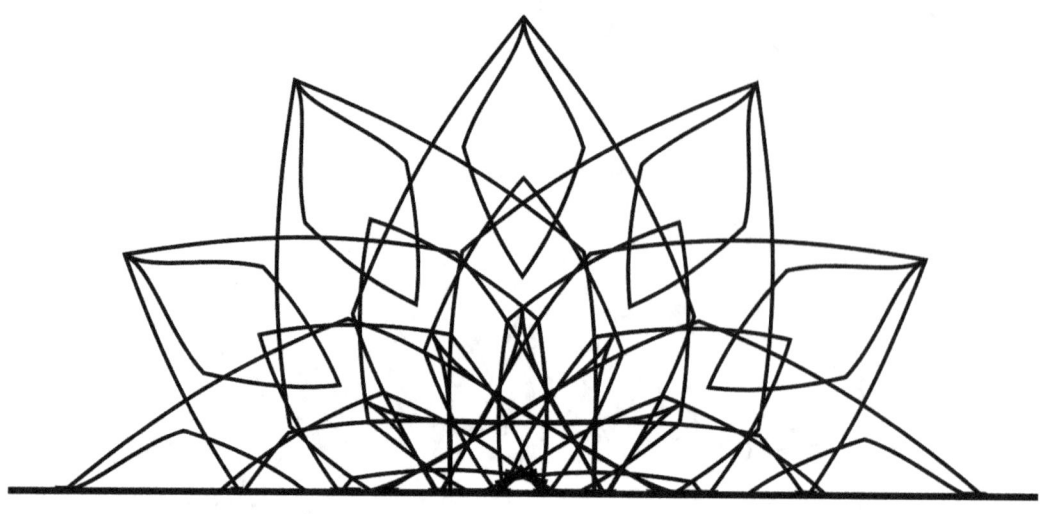

Labradors can be prone to obesity if they don't get enough exercise.

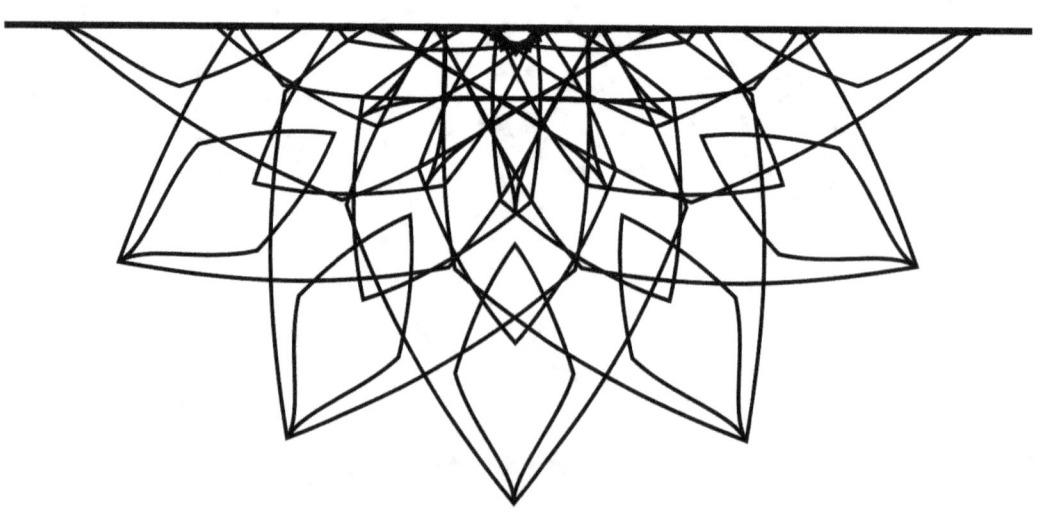

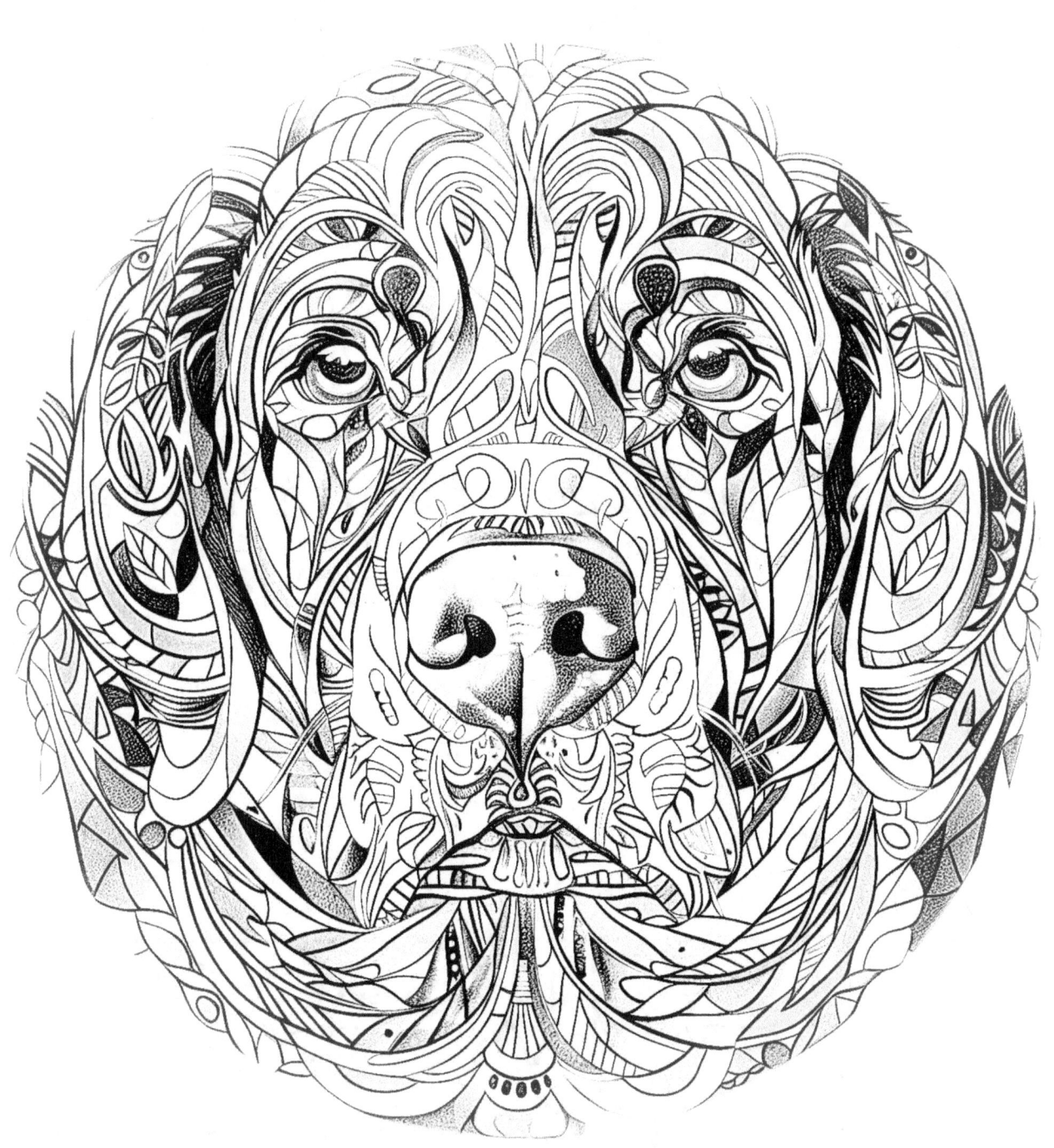

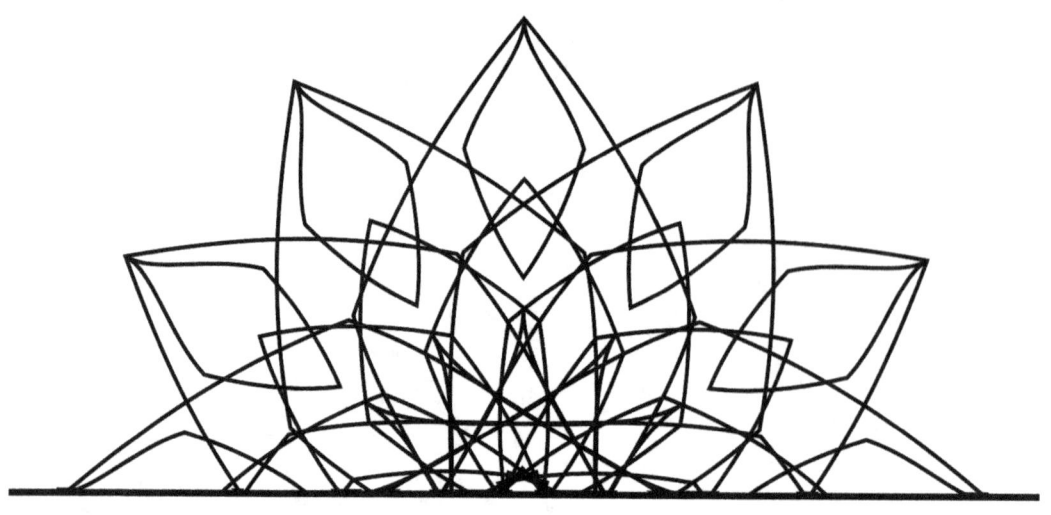

These dogs love getting attention and are often very sociable.

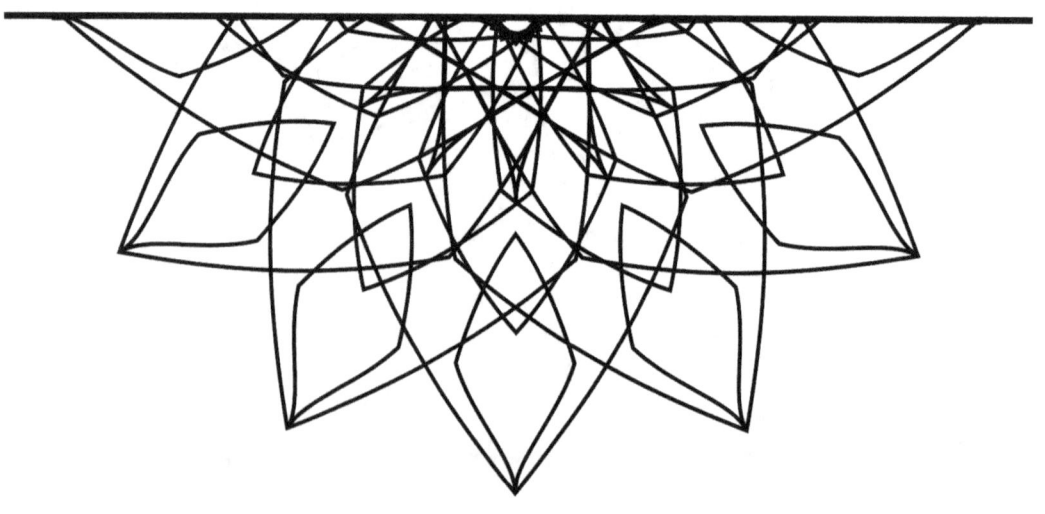

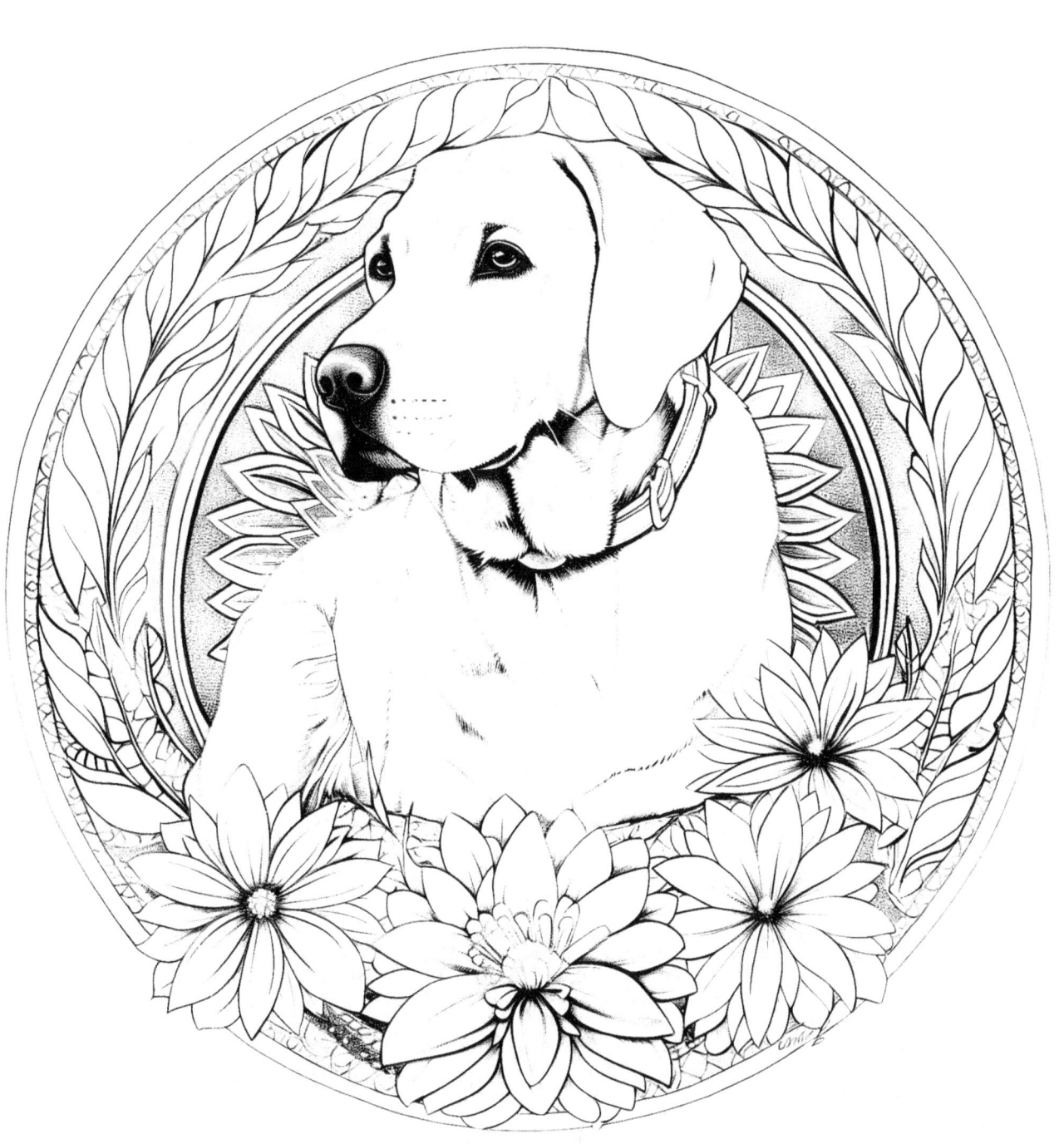

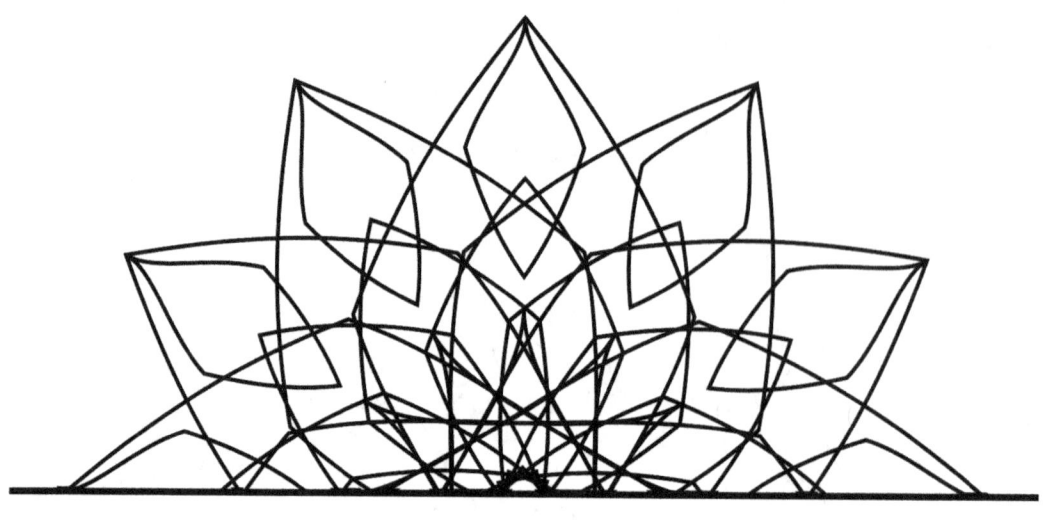

Labradors can form a strong bond with their owners and are considered loyal companions.

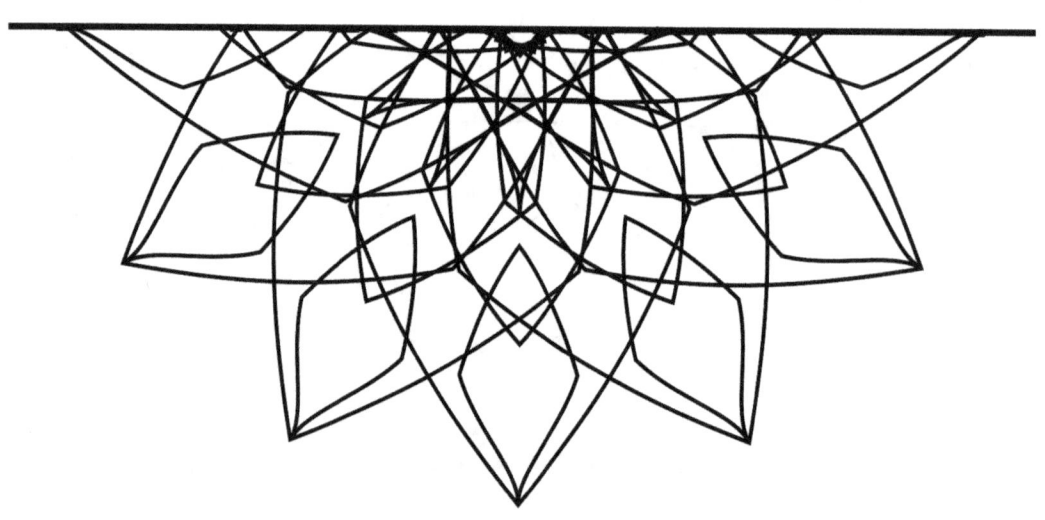

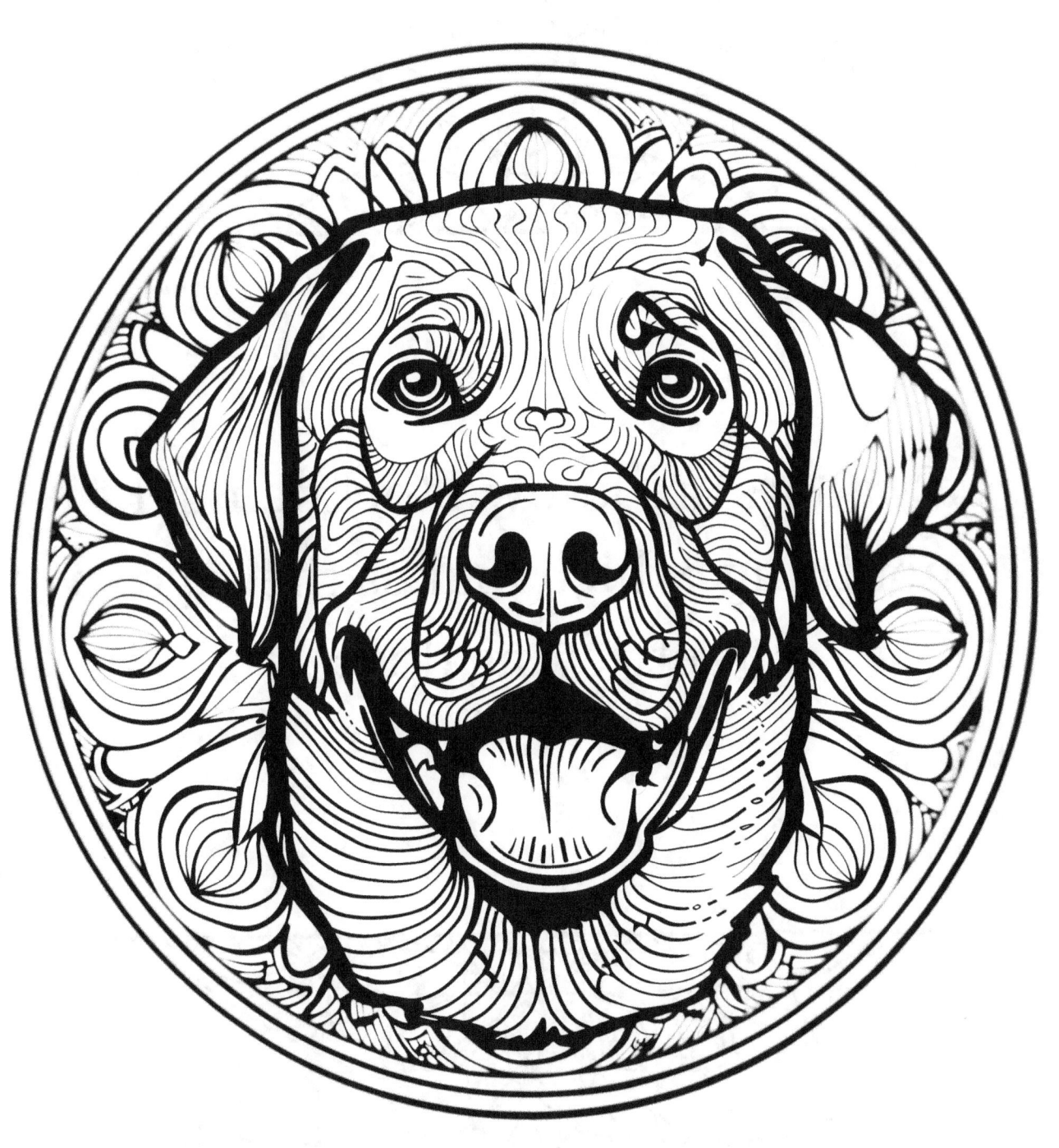

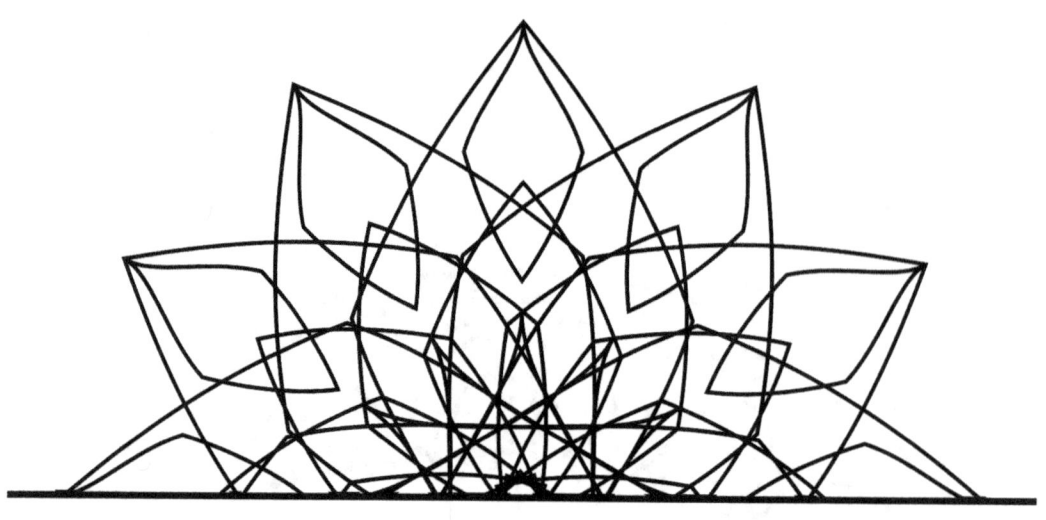

Labradors are known for their gentle mouthing, which makes them good retrieving dogs.

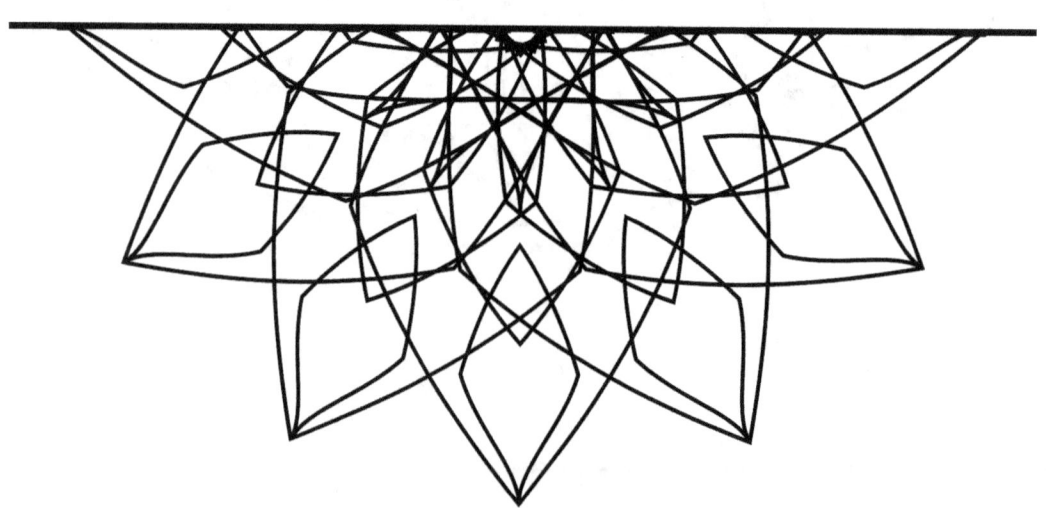

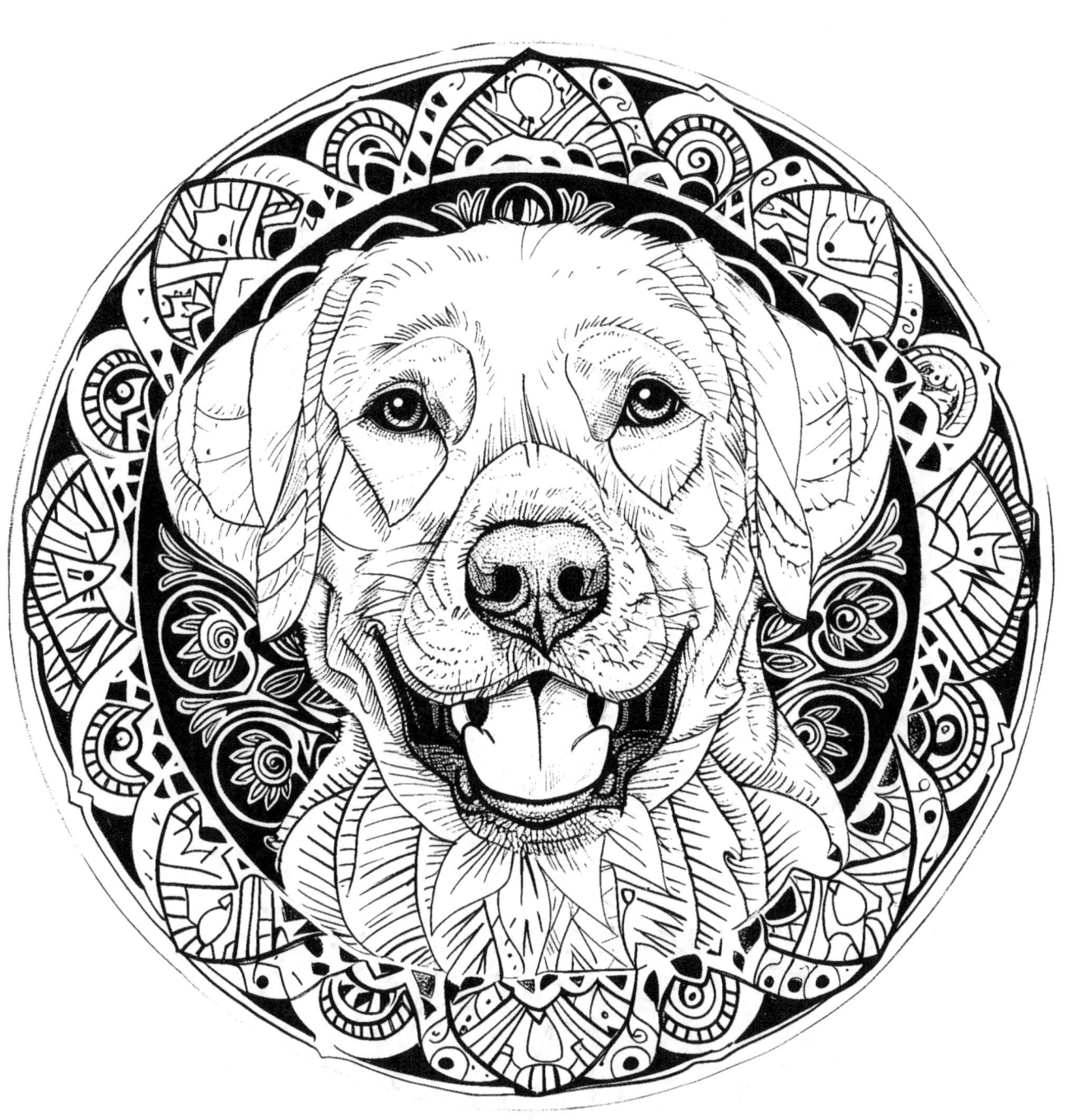

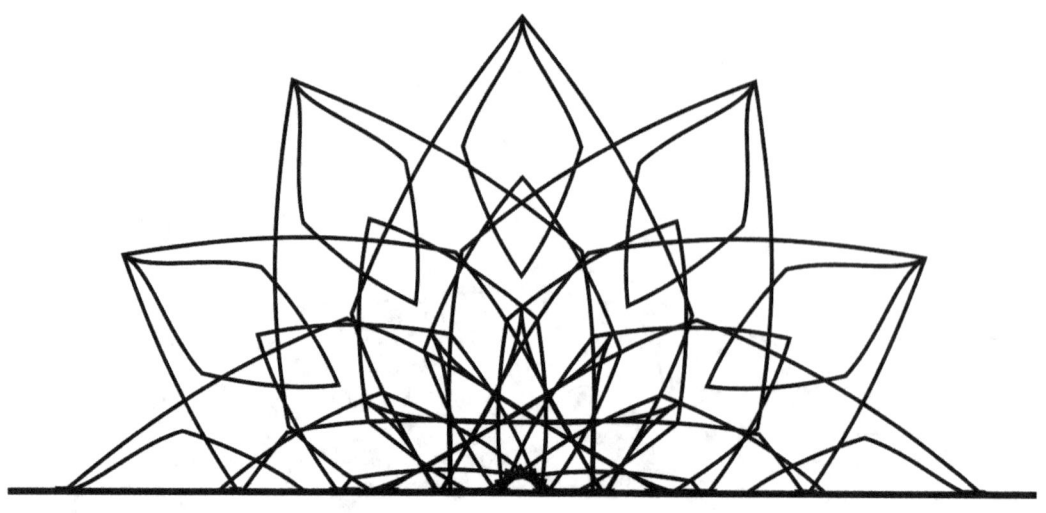

They have a double coat that protects them from various weather conditions.

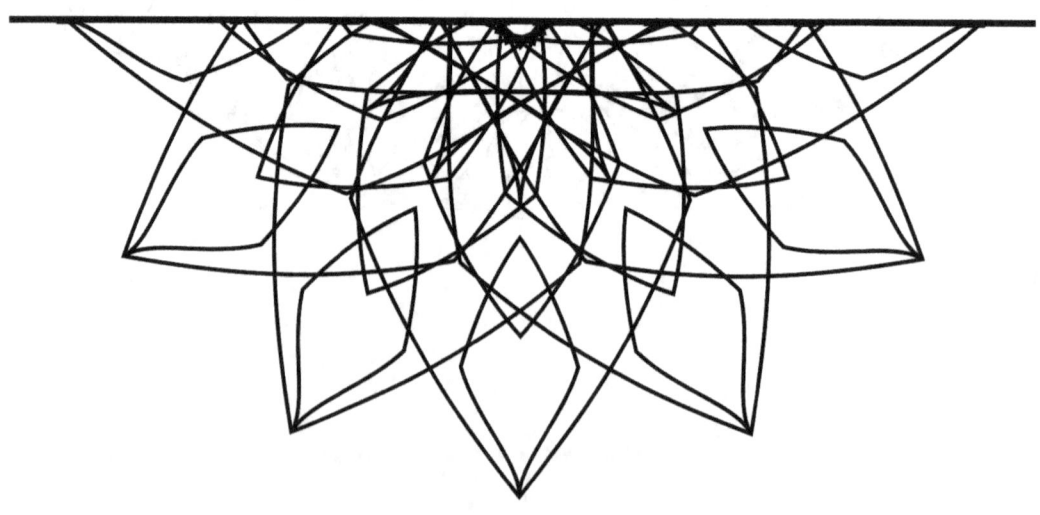

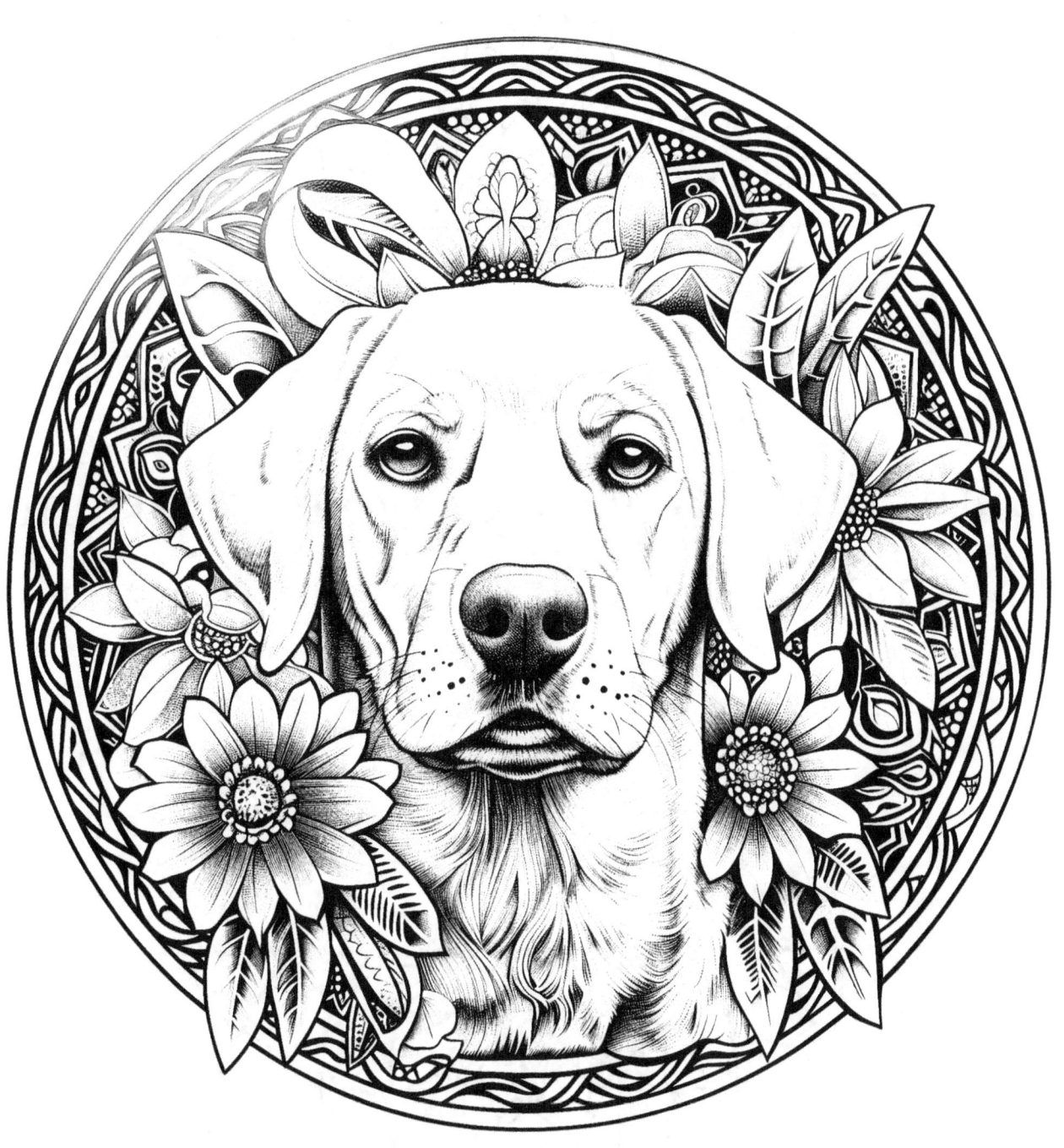

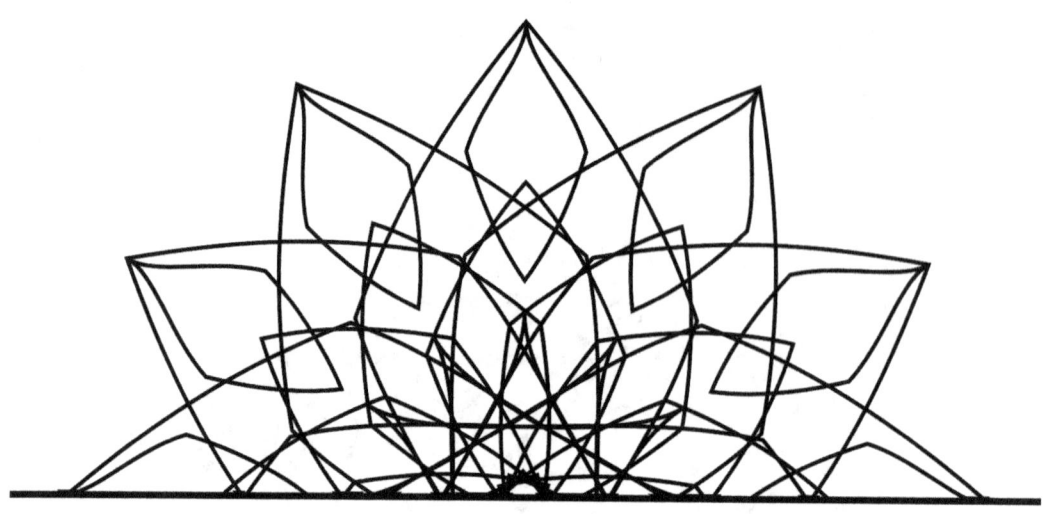

Labradors are generally very patient and tolerant of other animals.

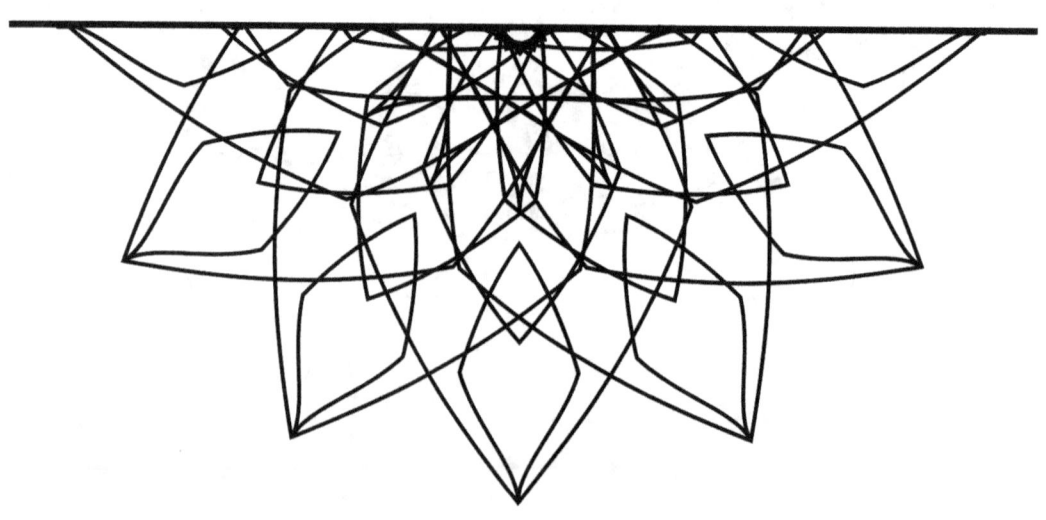

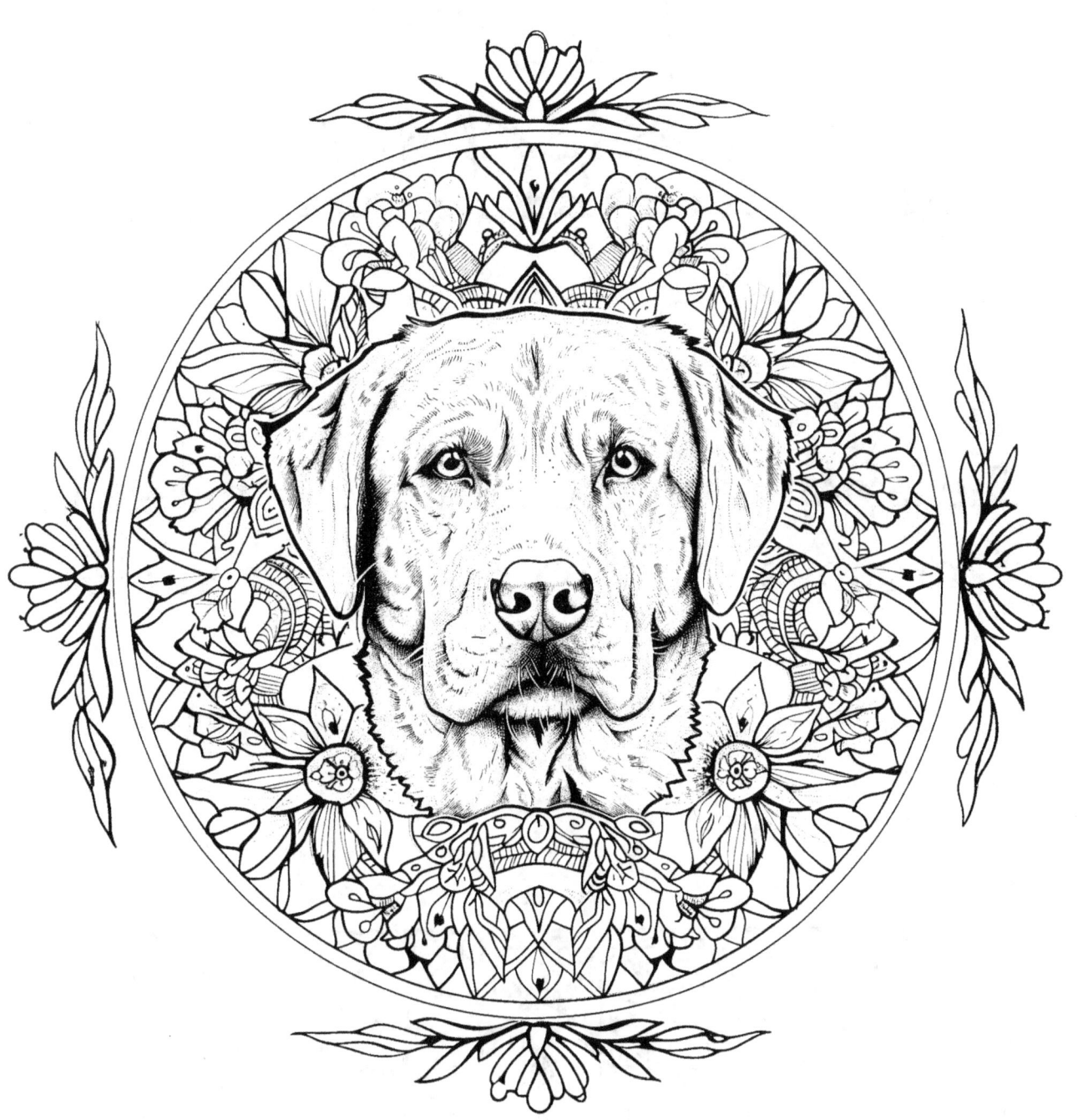

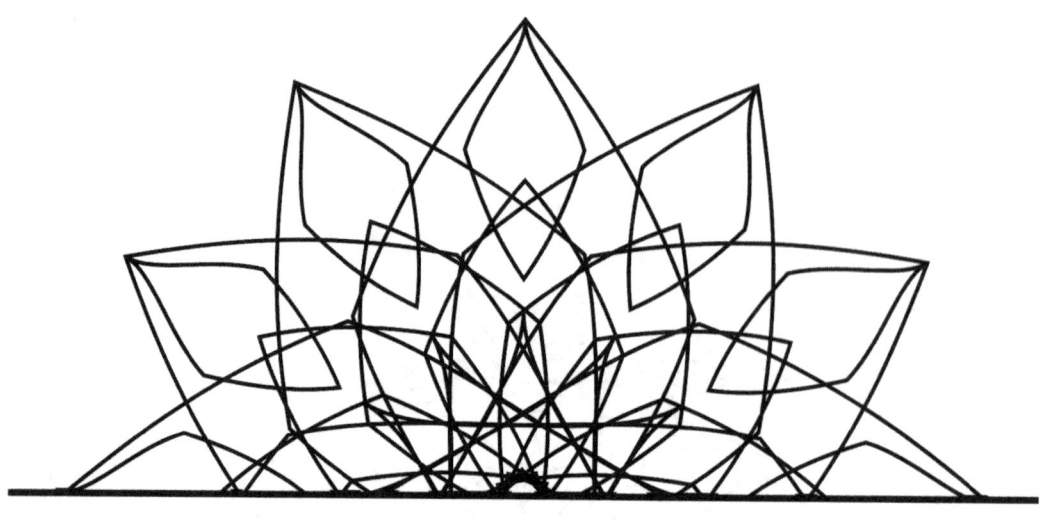

These dogs are often involved in rescue missions and have excellent search ability.

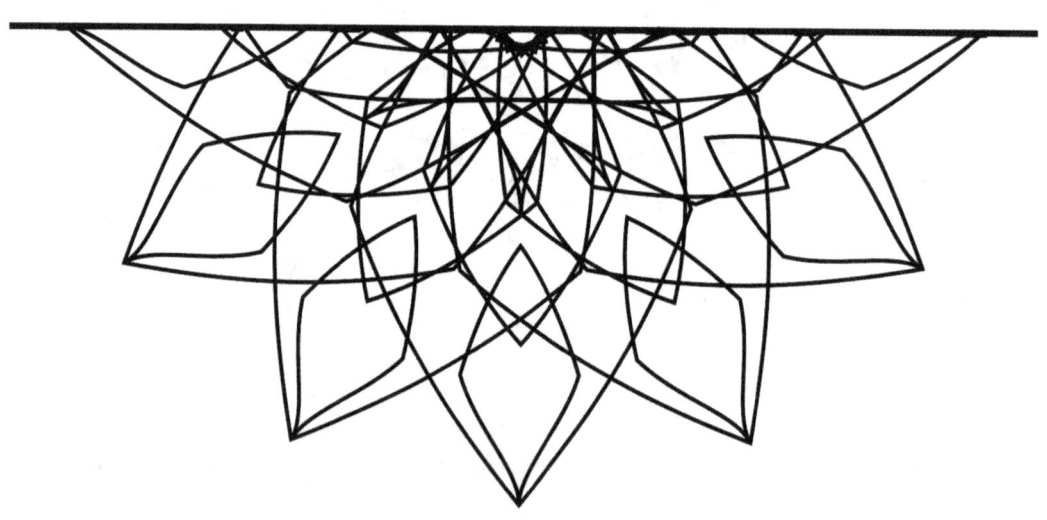

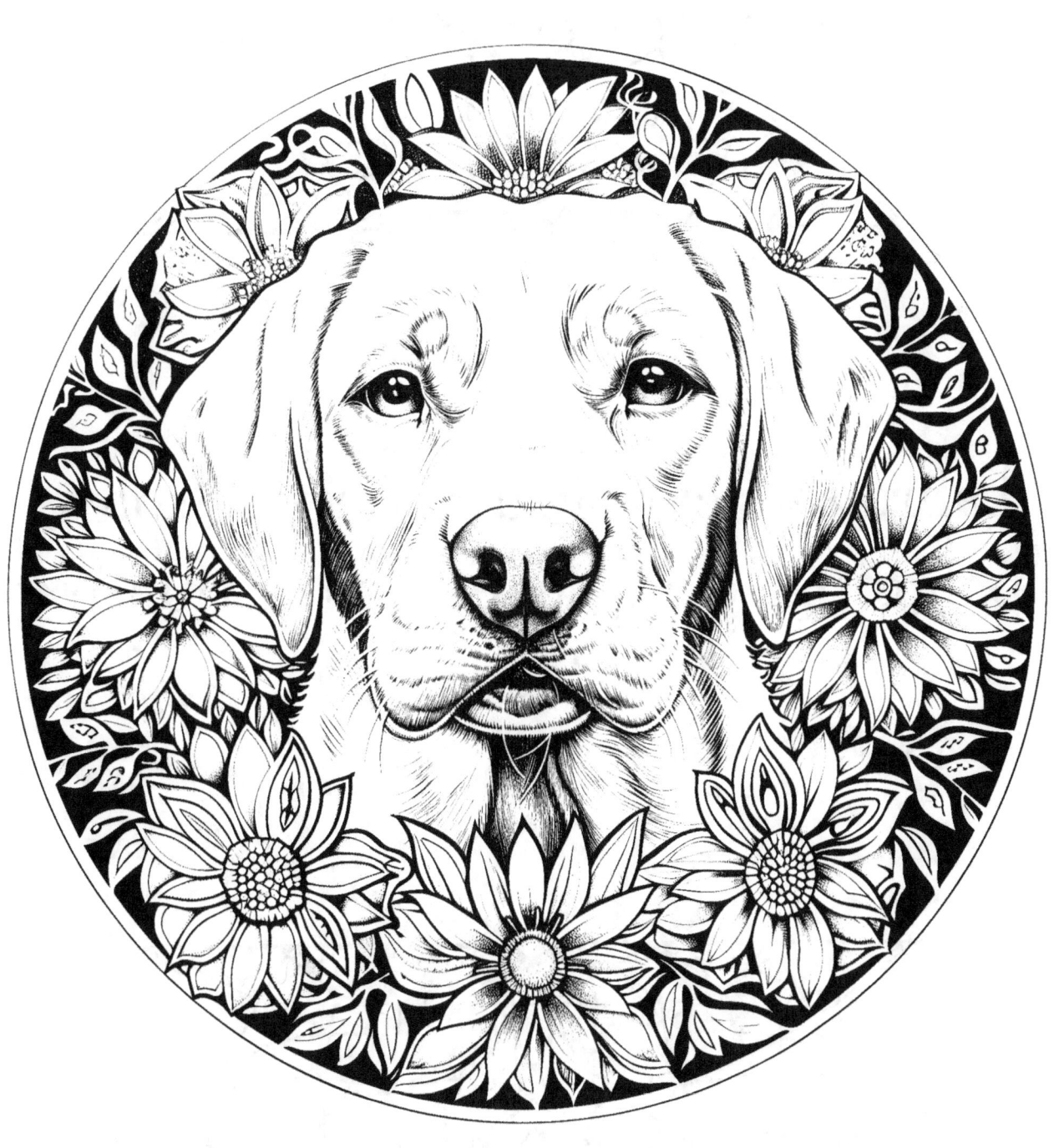

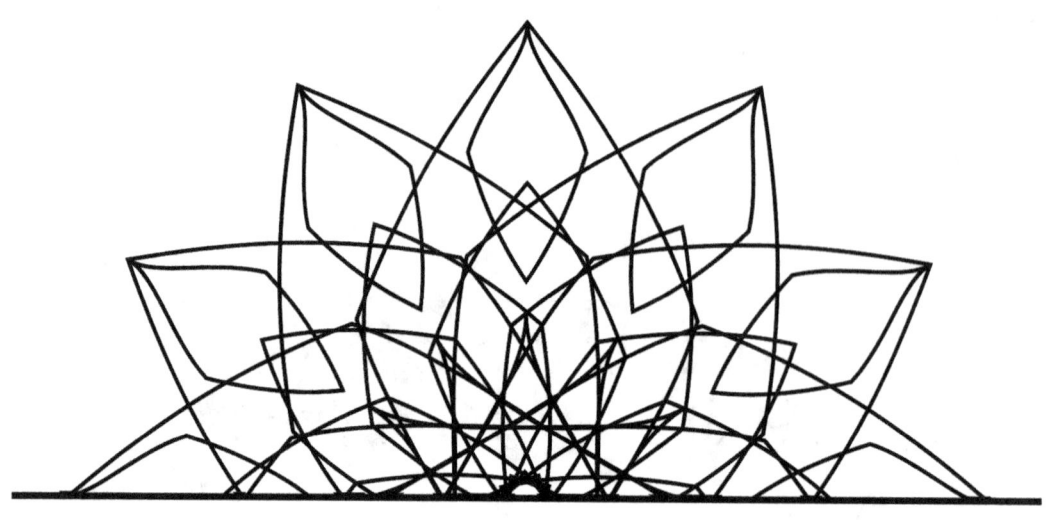

Labradors can fill a variety of roles, including seeing-eye dogs or therapy dogs.

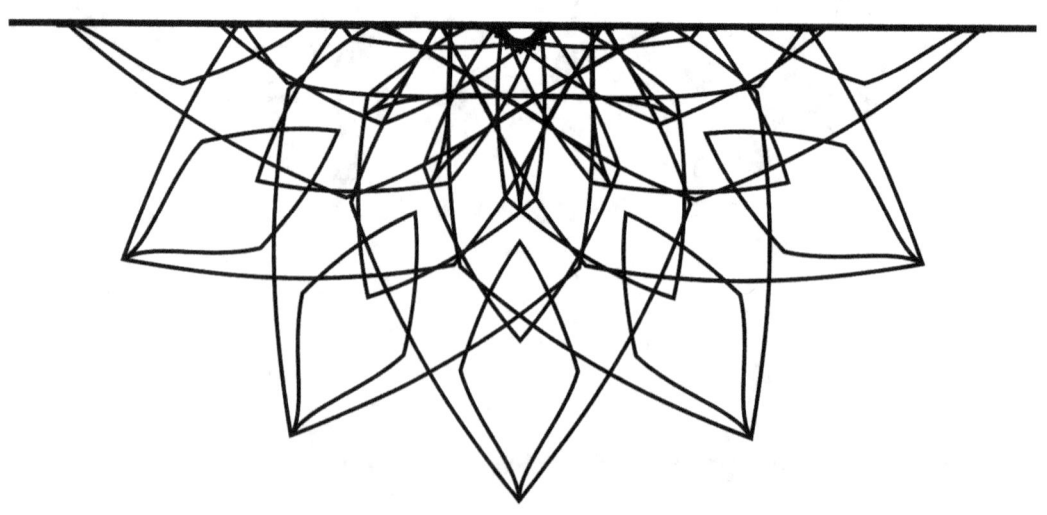

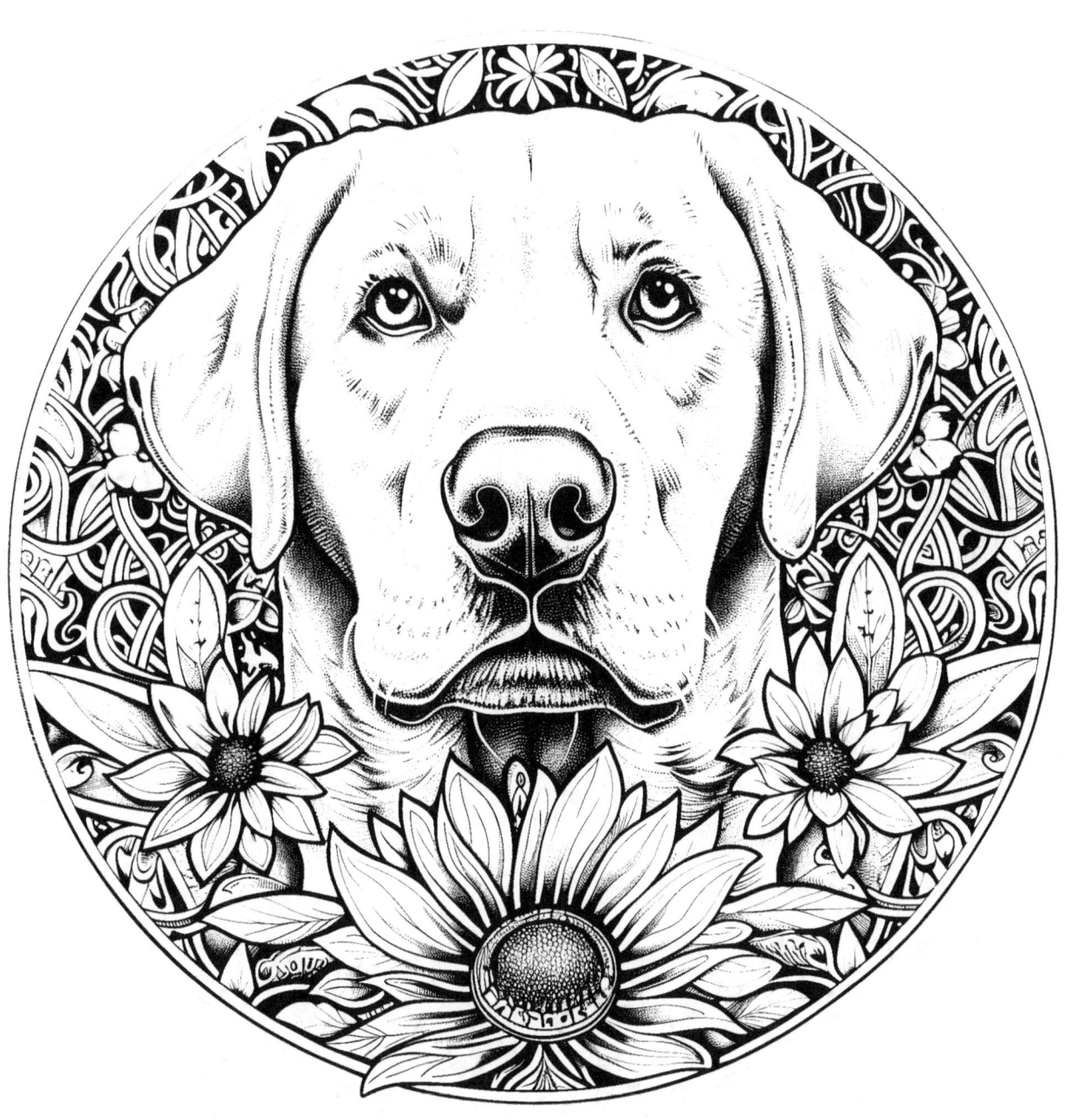

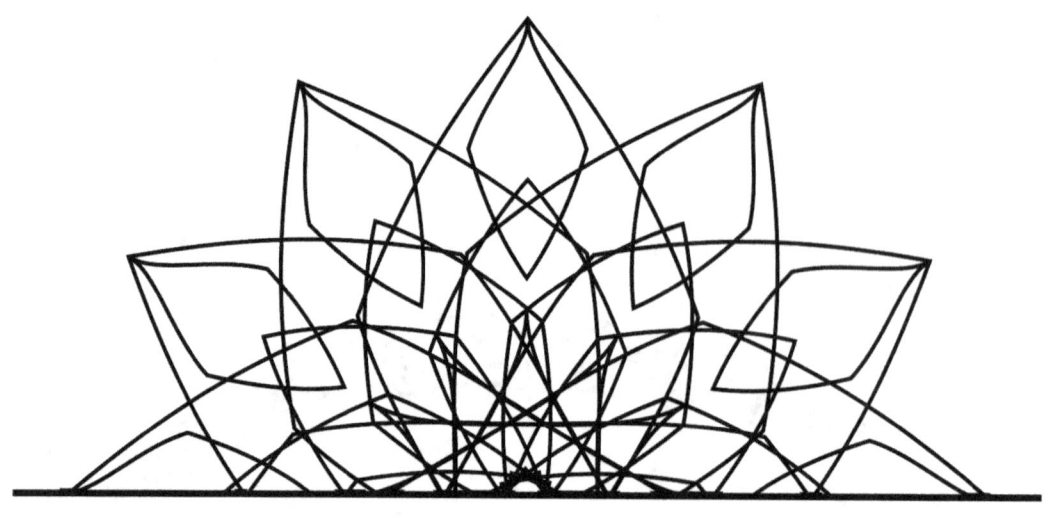

They are extremely social and enjoy the company of people and other dogs.

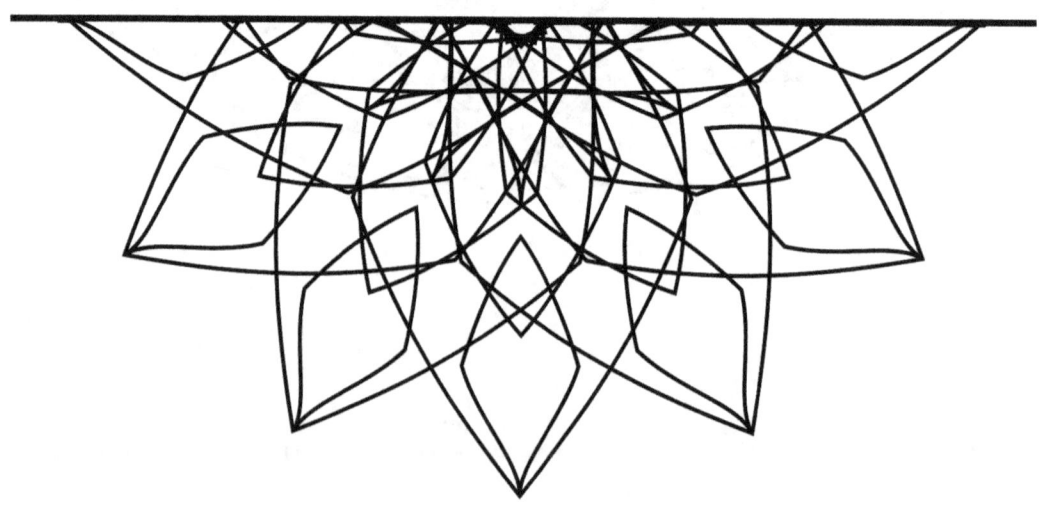

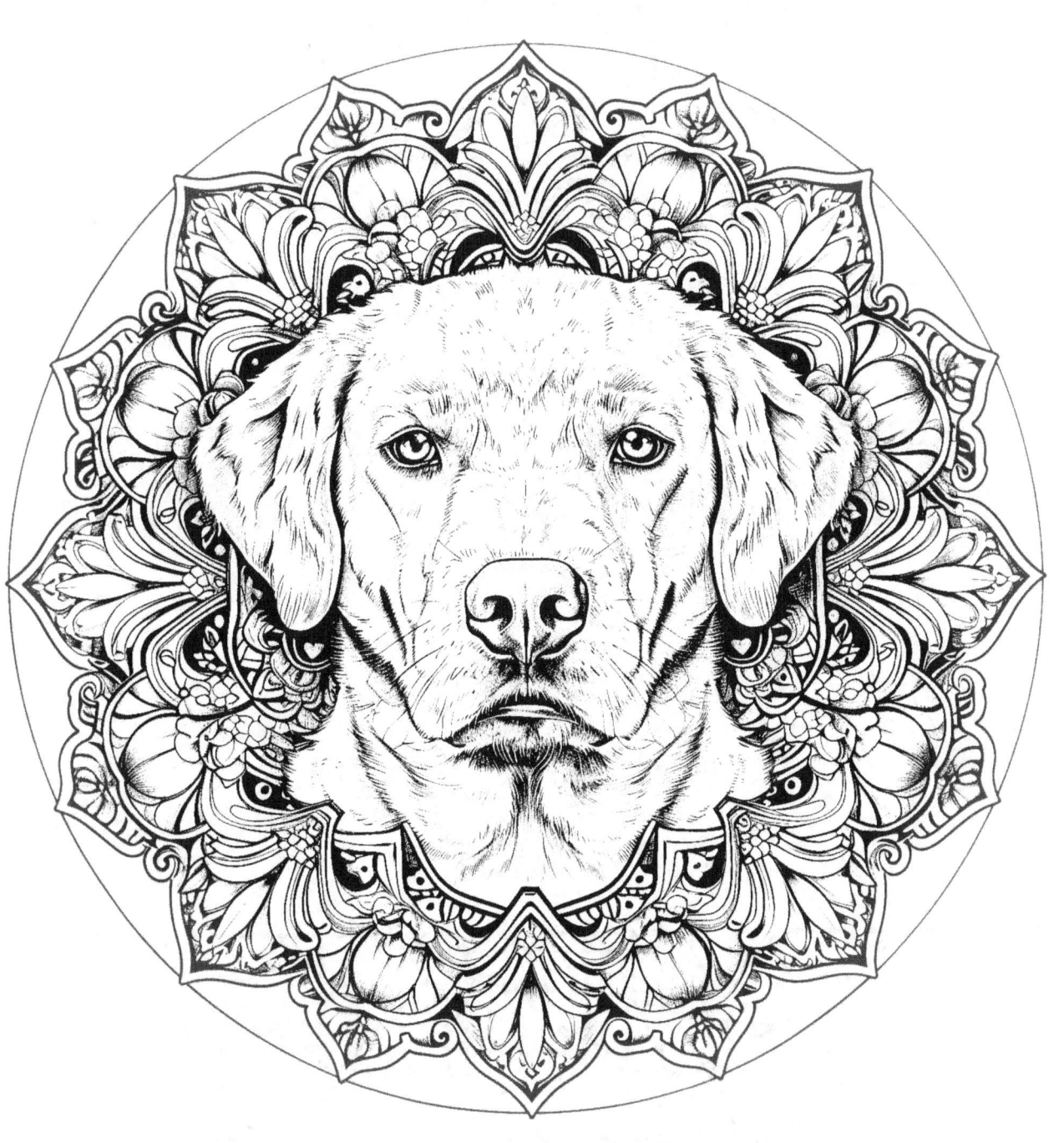

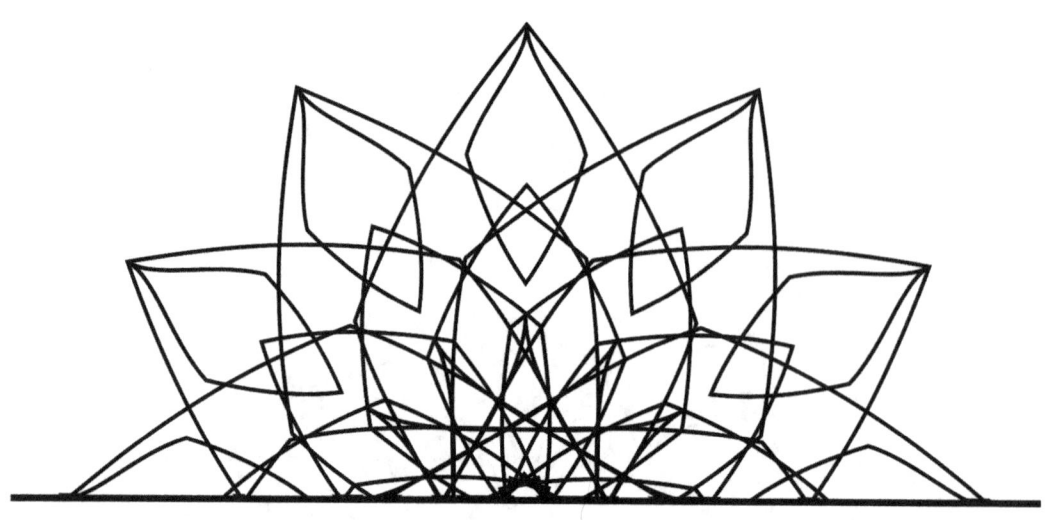

Labradors can reach an impressive top speed of up to 48km/h (30mph).

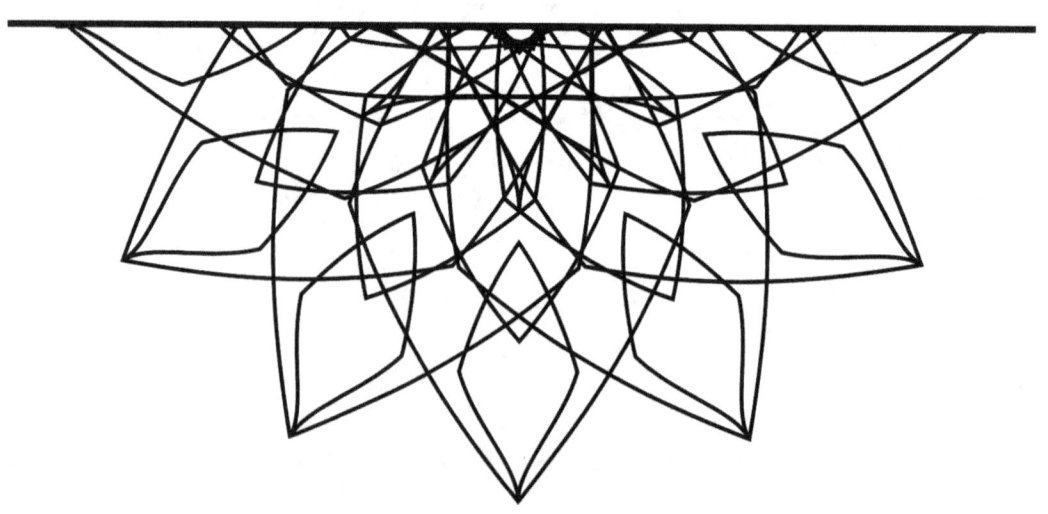

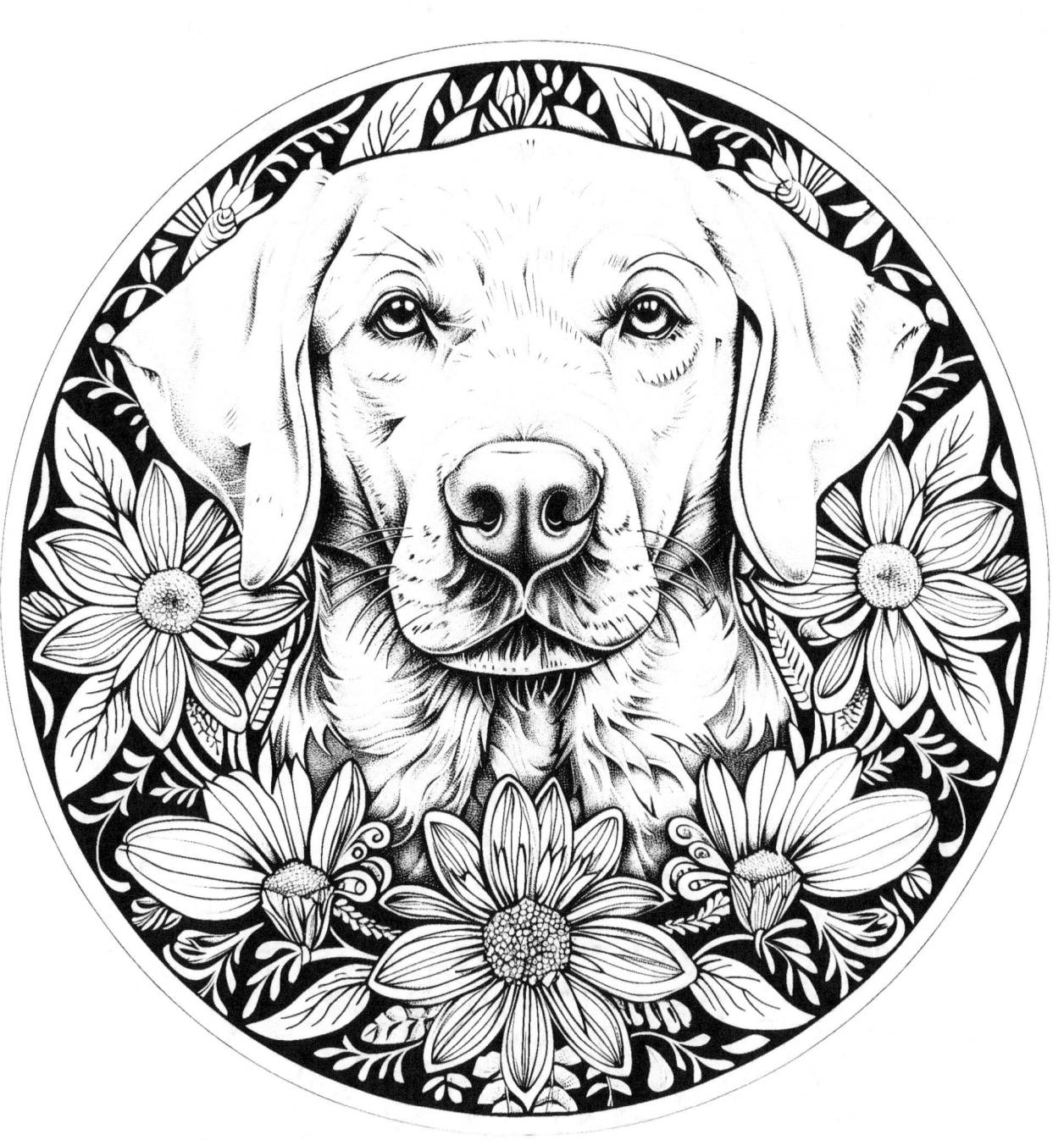

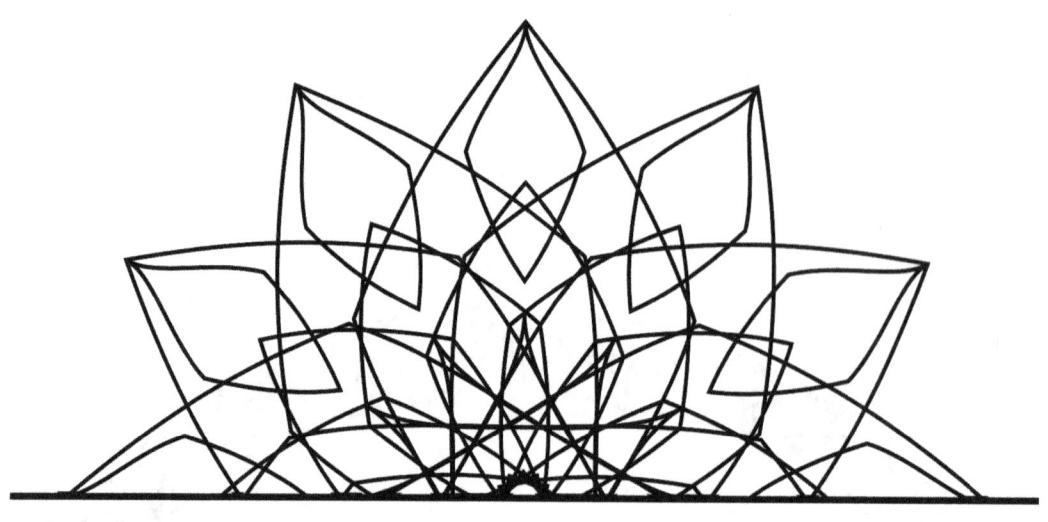

The breed is known for having a strong work ethic and loves completing tasks.

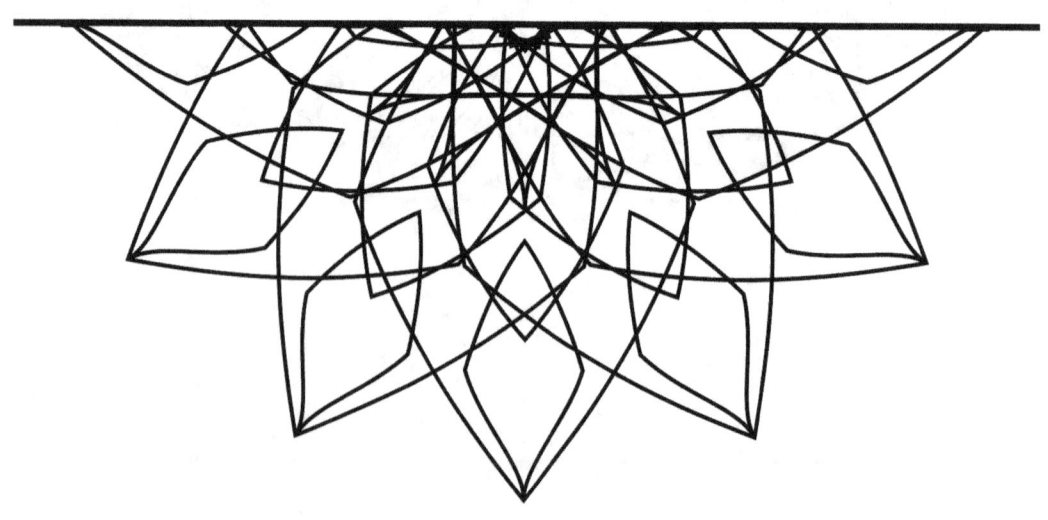

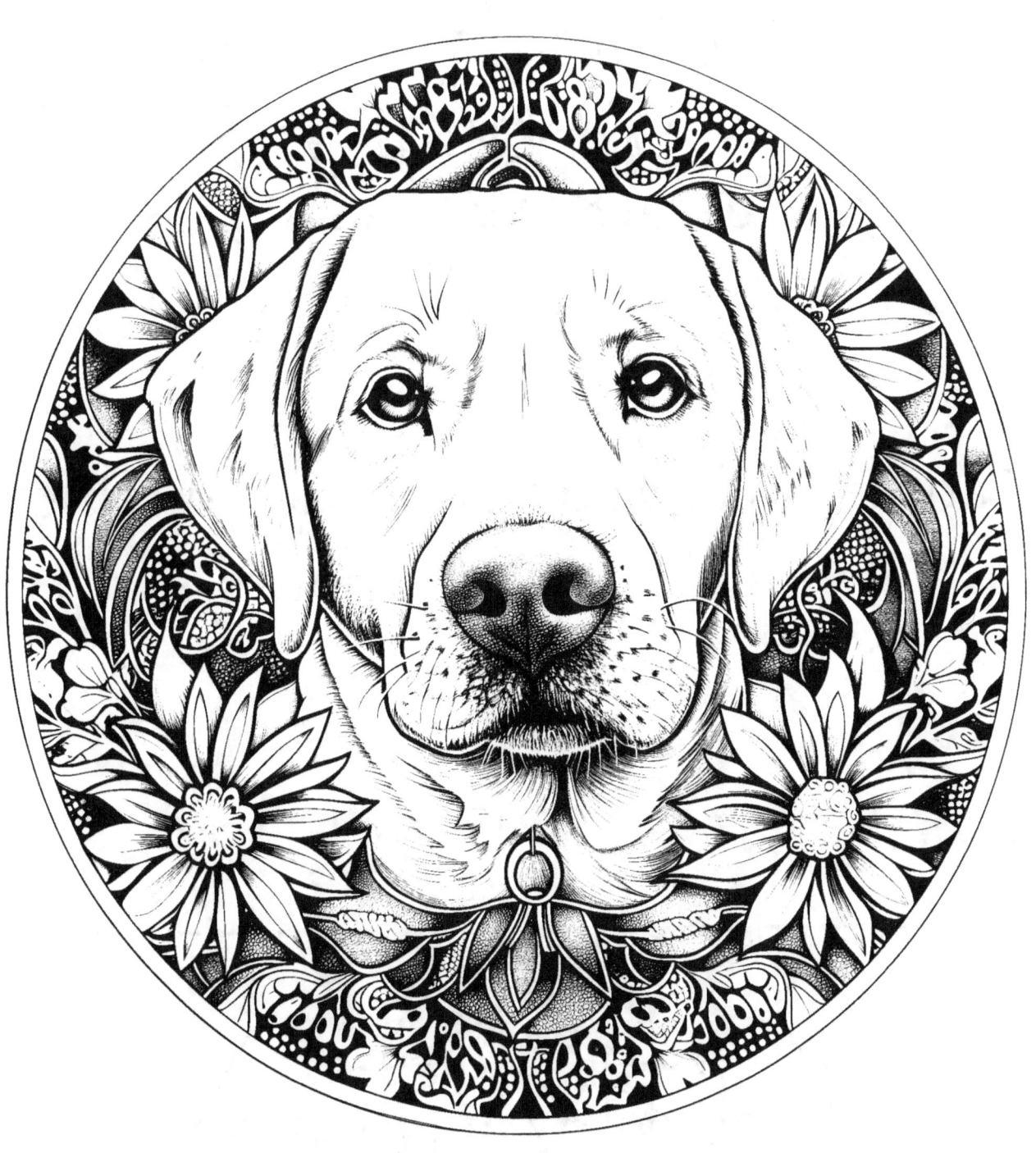

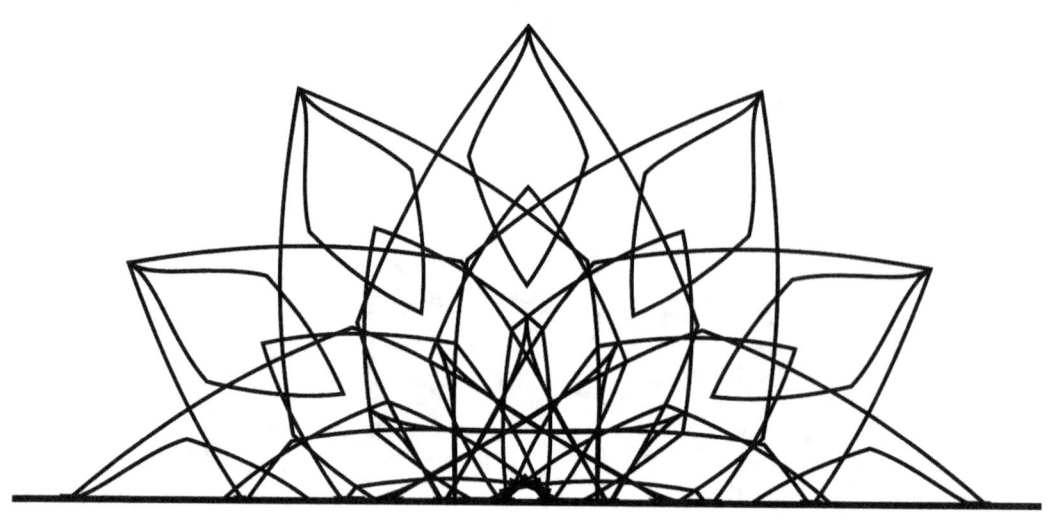

Labradors have a strong play instinct and can play for hours.

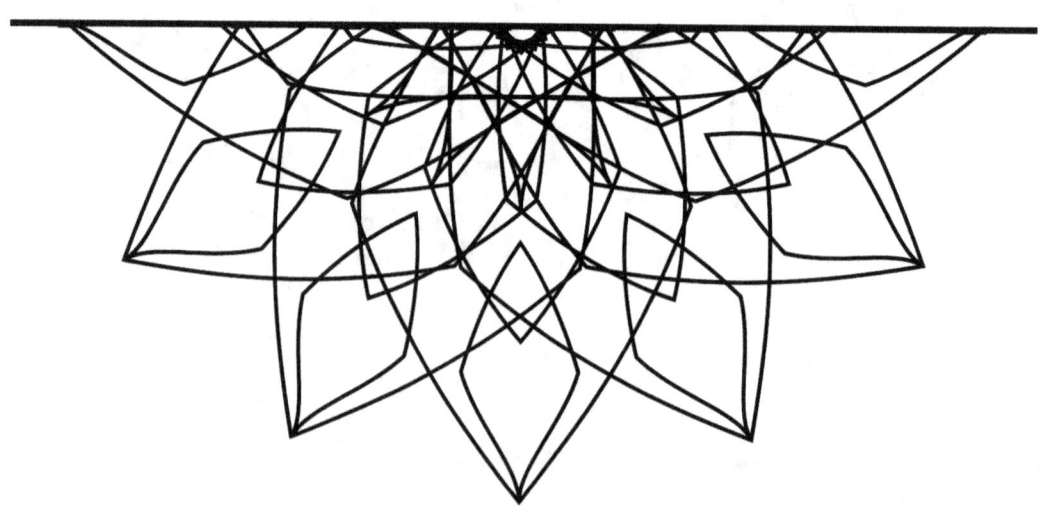

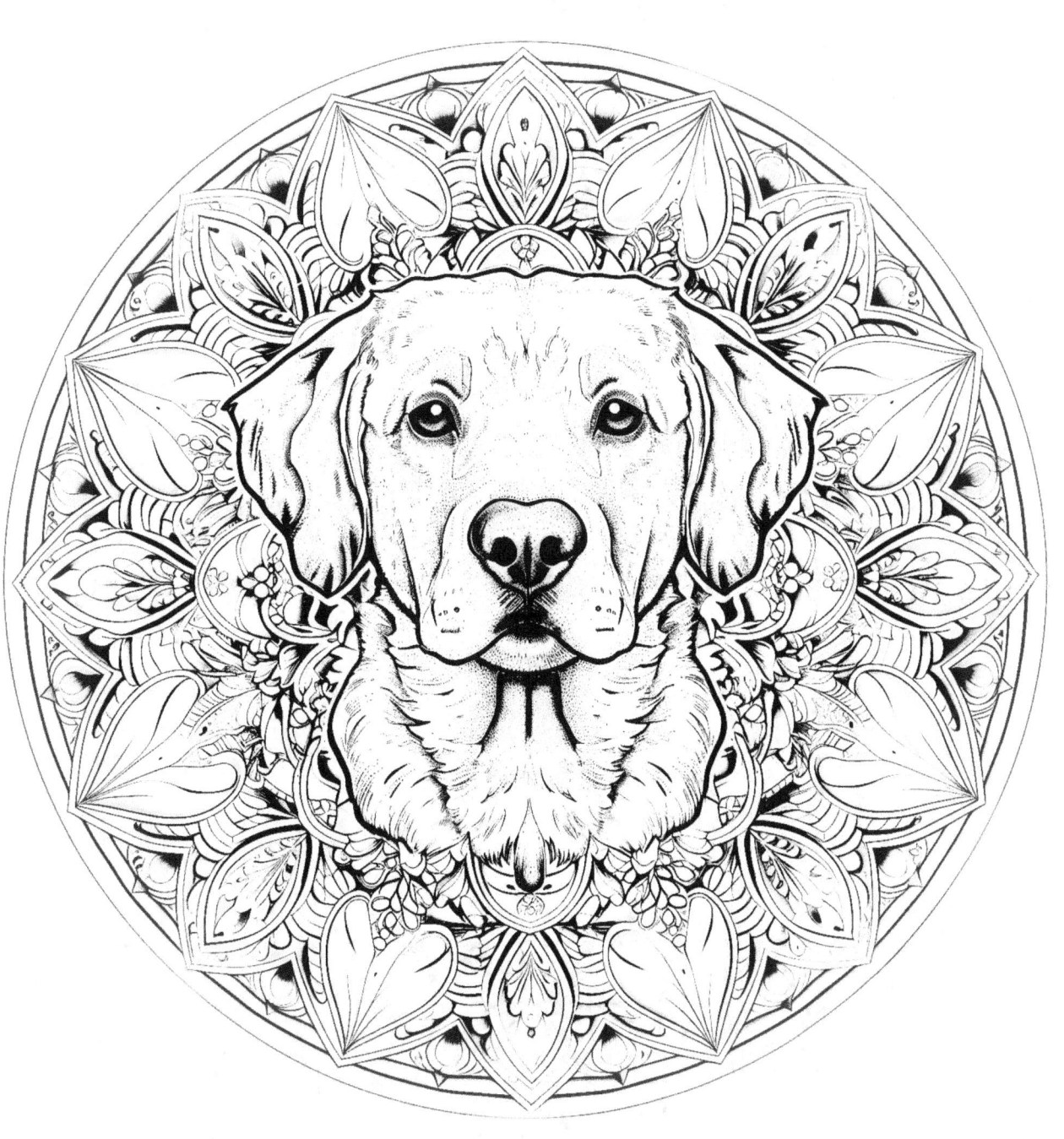

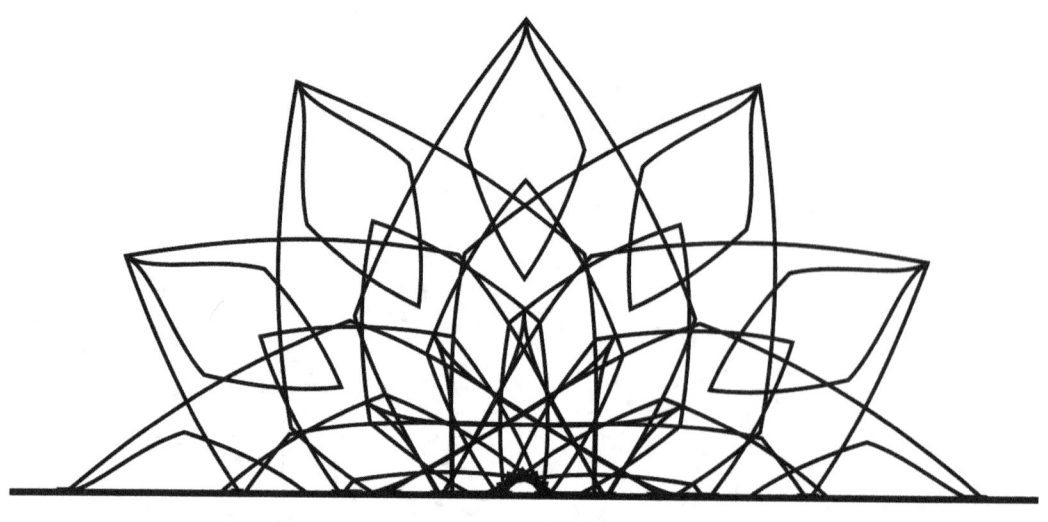

They are adaptable and can live in different environments, from rural to urban.

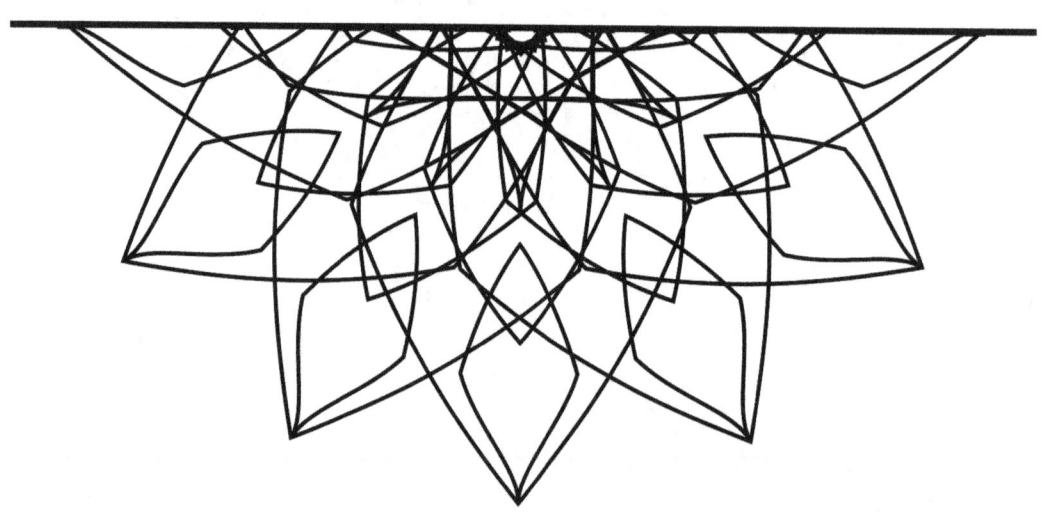

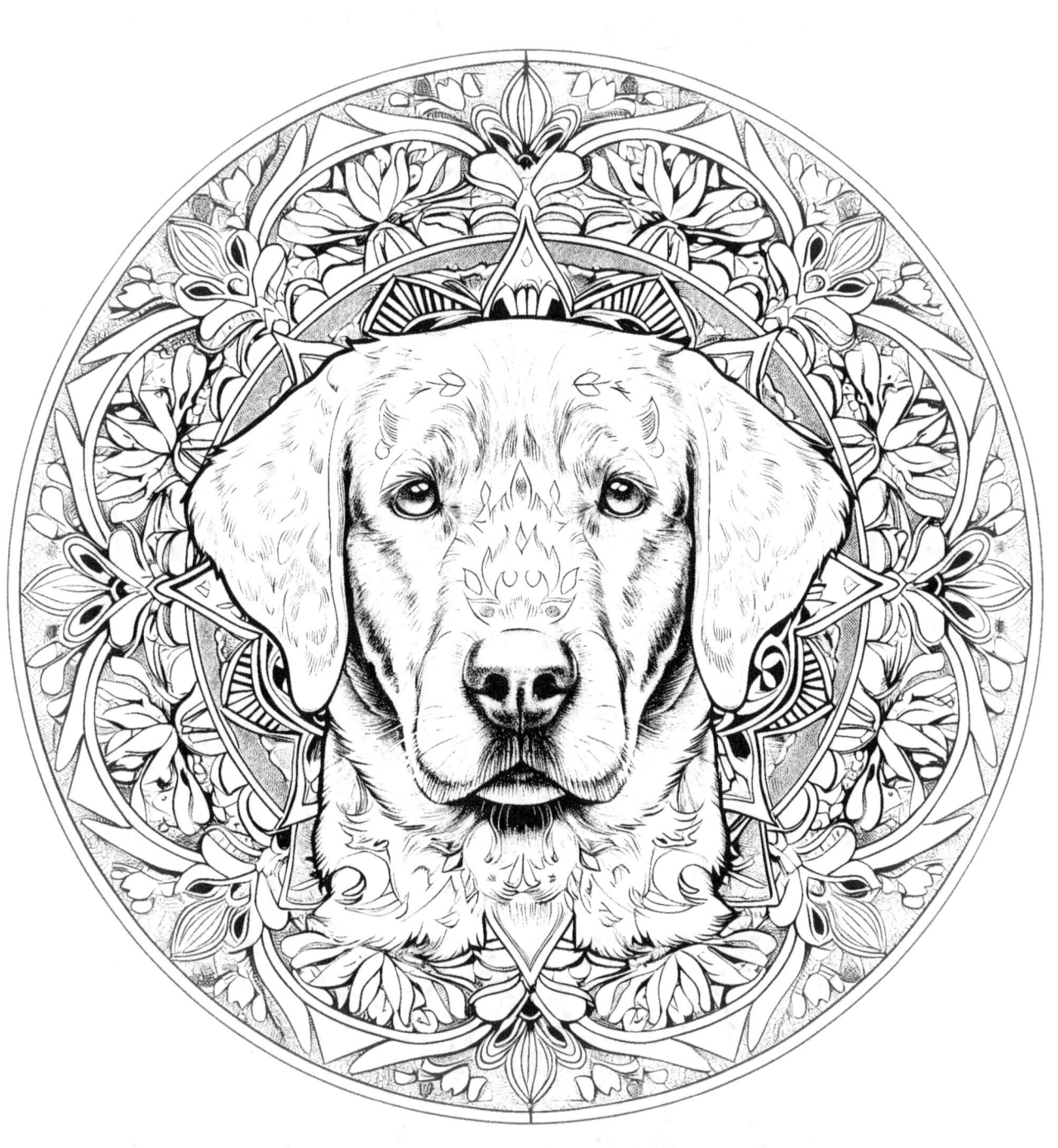

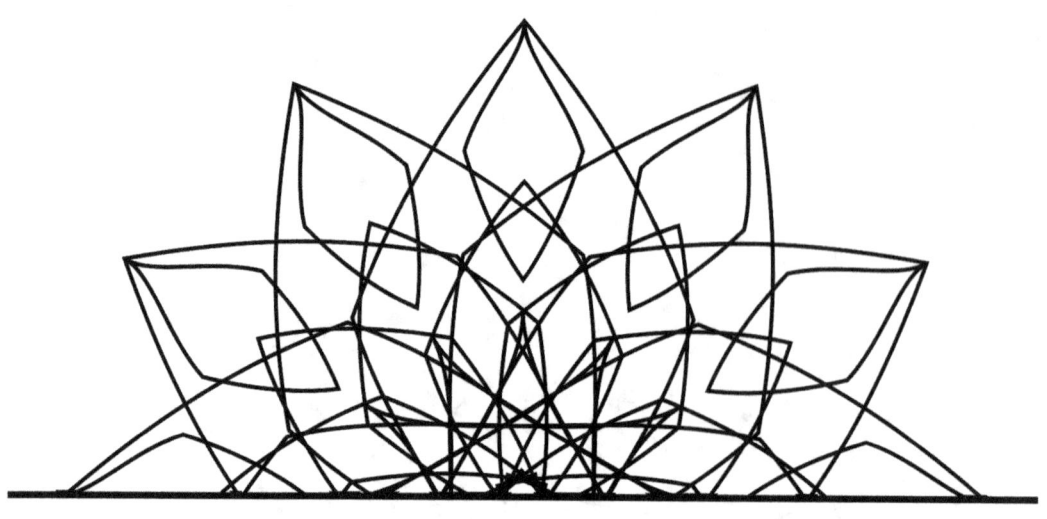

Labradors have strong swimming ability and can cope well in cold water.

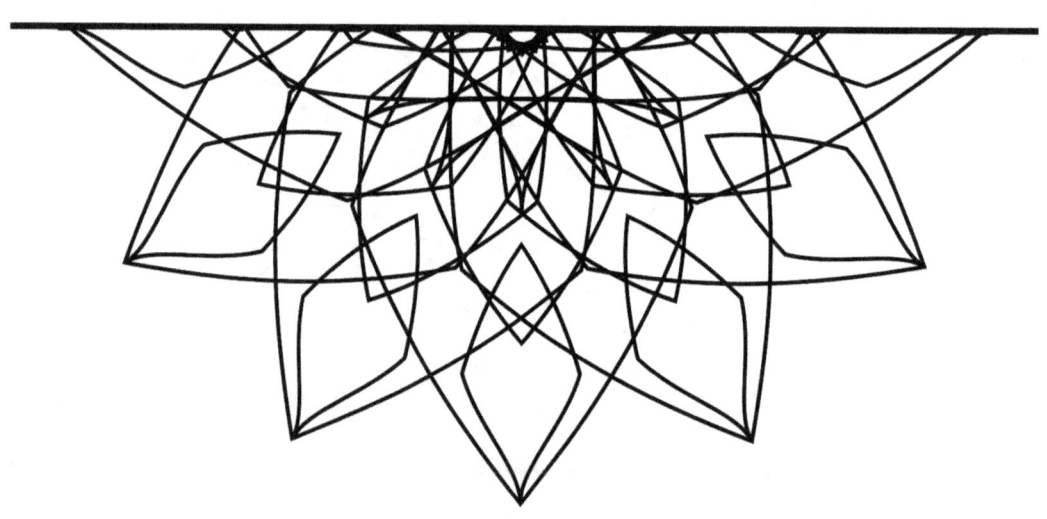

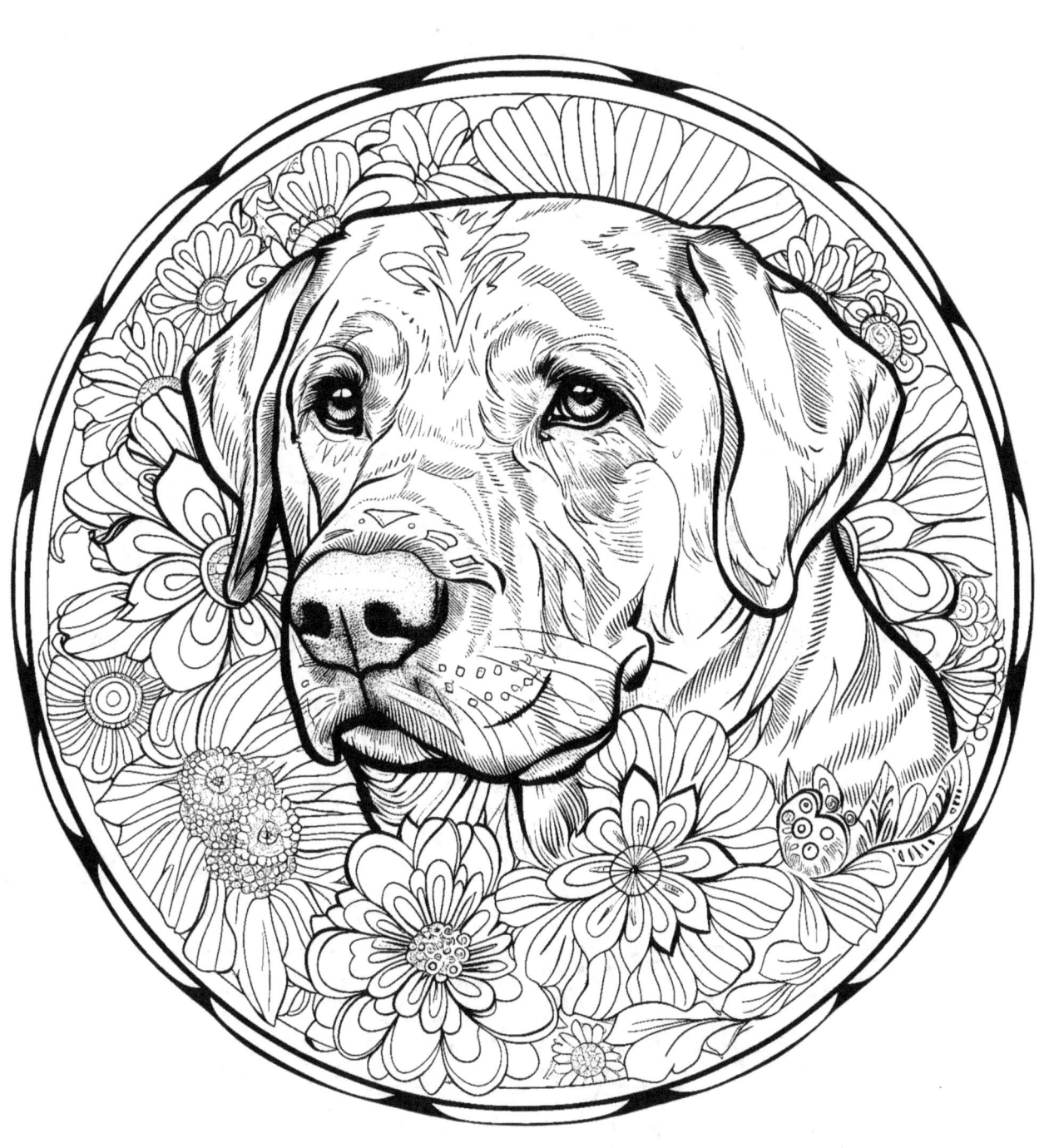

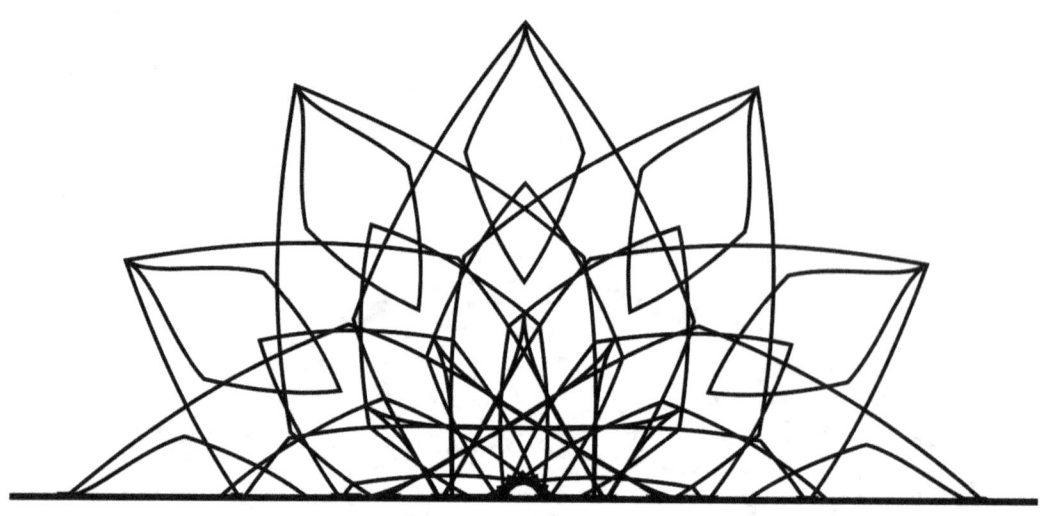

They are often seen in films and television shows due to their charming looks and intelligence.

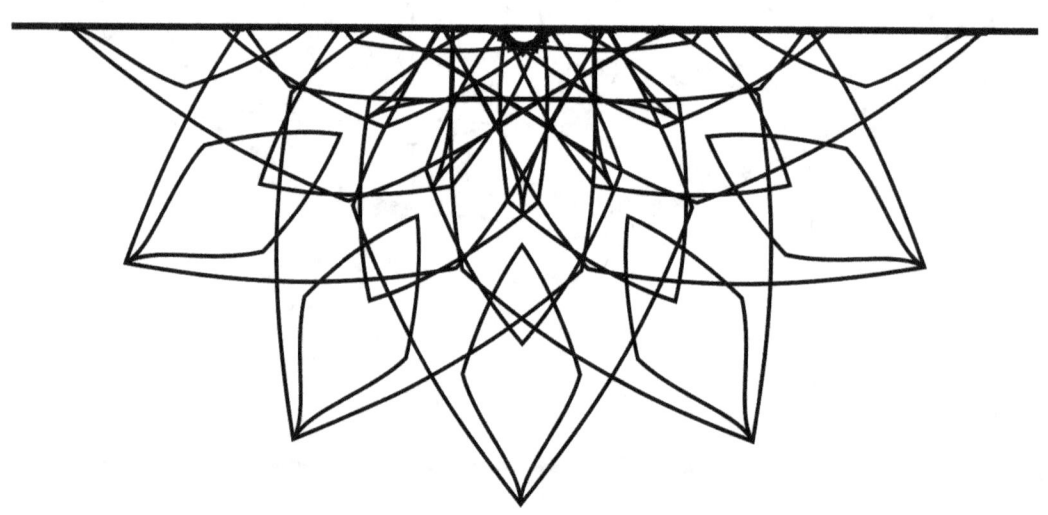

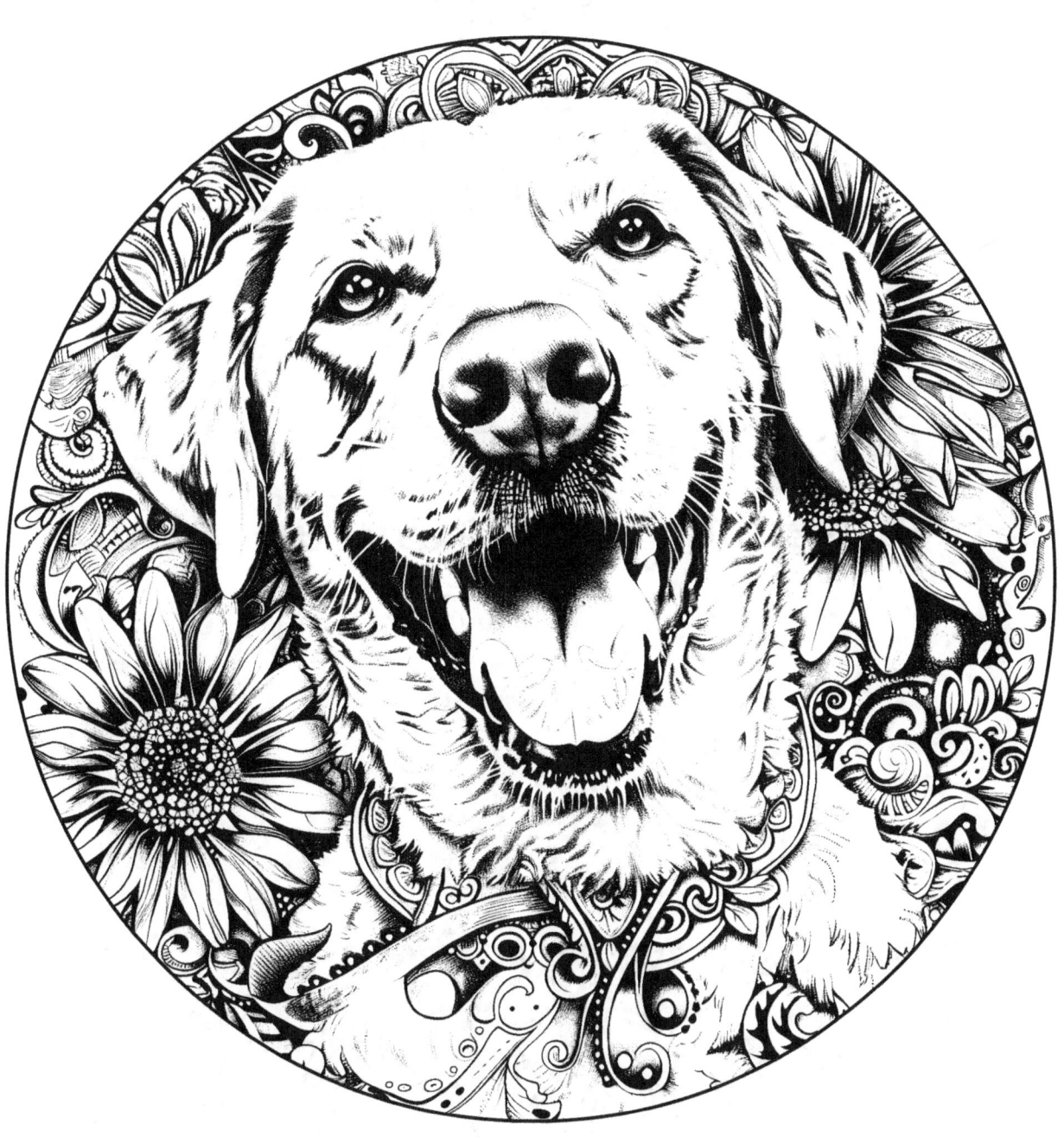

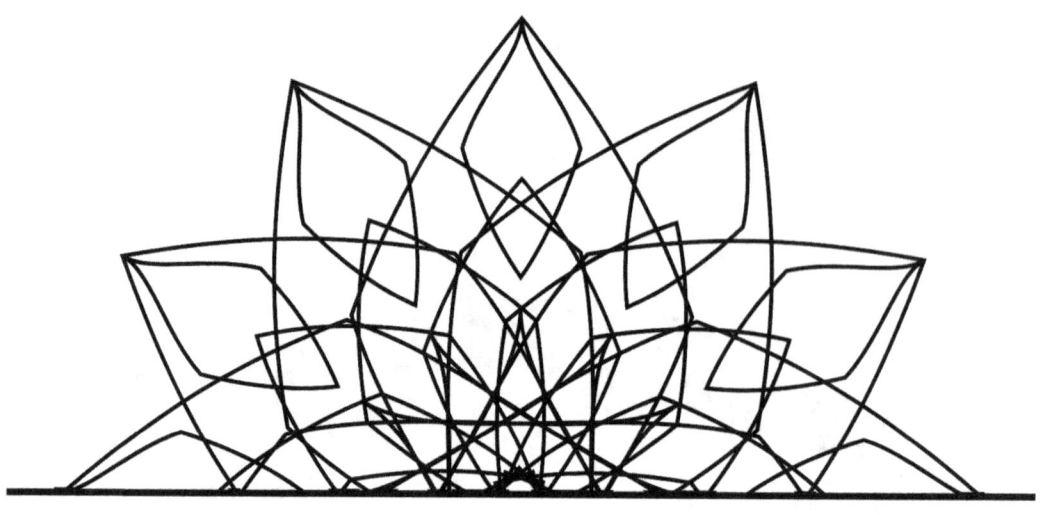

These dogs can have a strong preference for toys and are often referred to as "towline thieves."

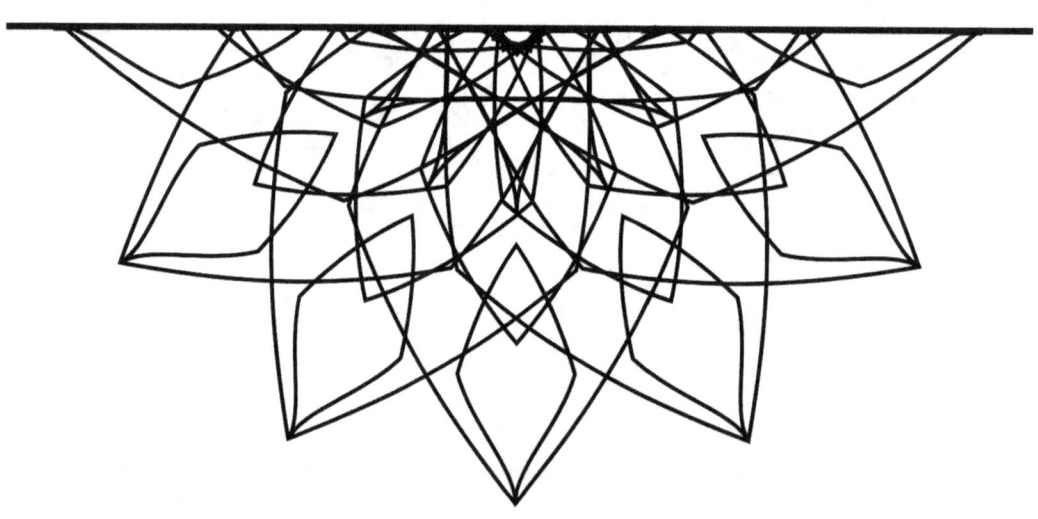

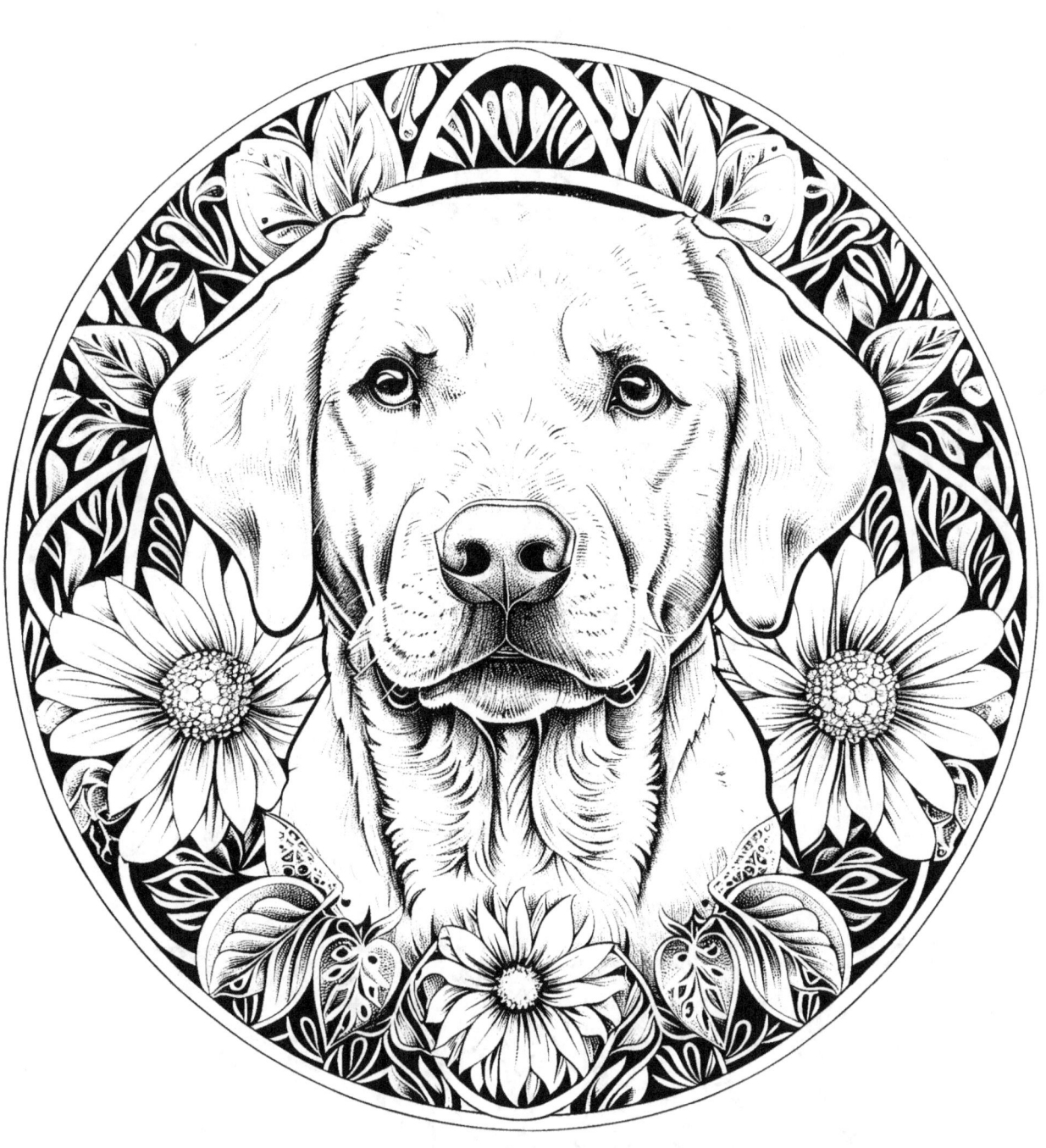

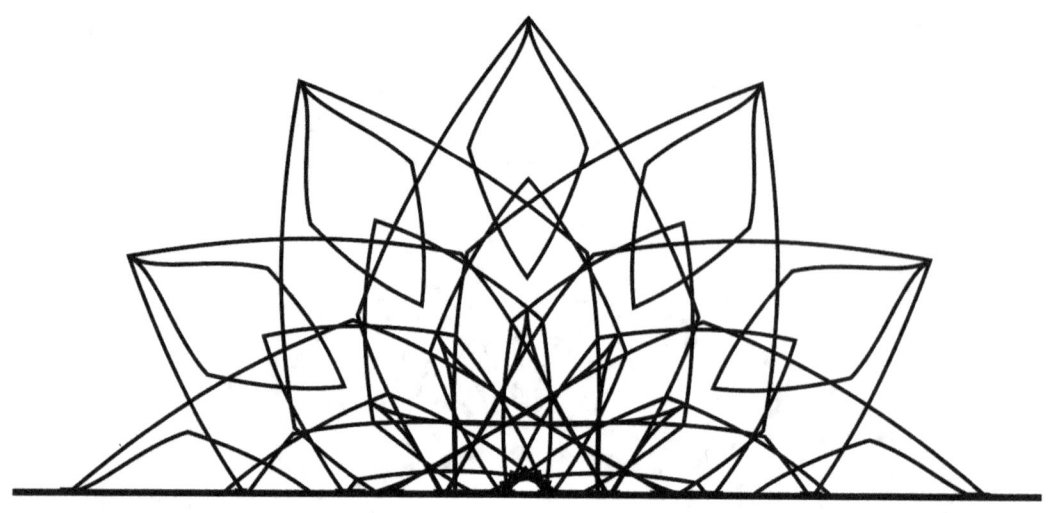

Labradors have a remarkable ability to adapt to their owners' emotions and provide comfort.

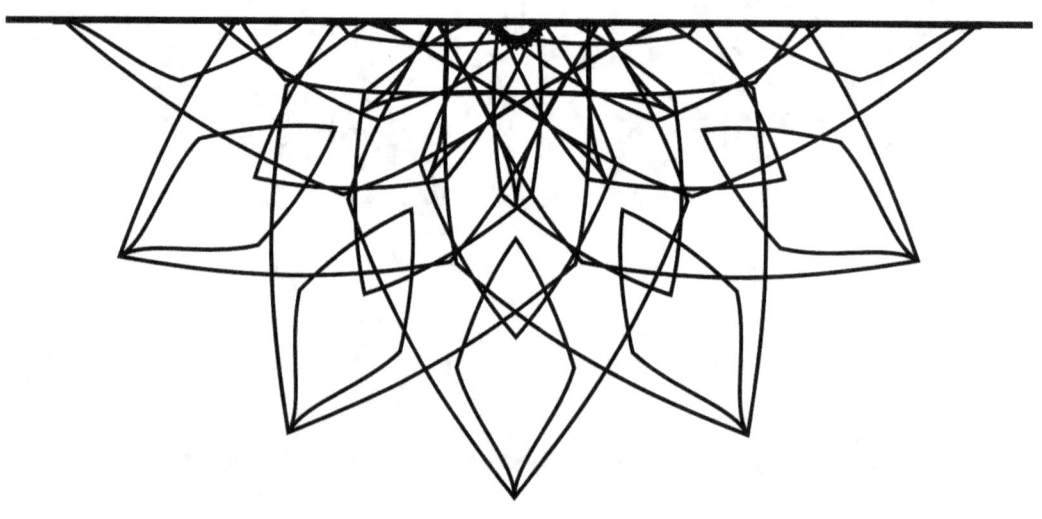

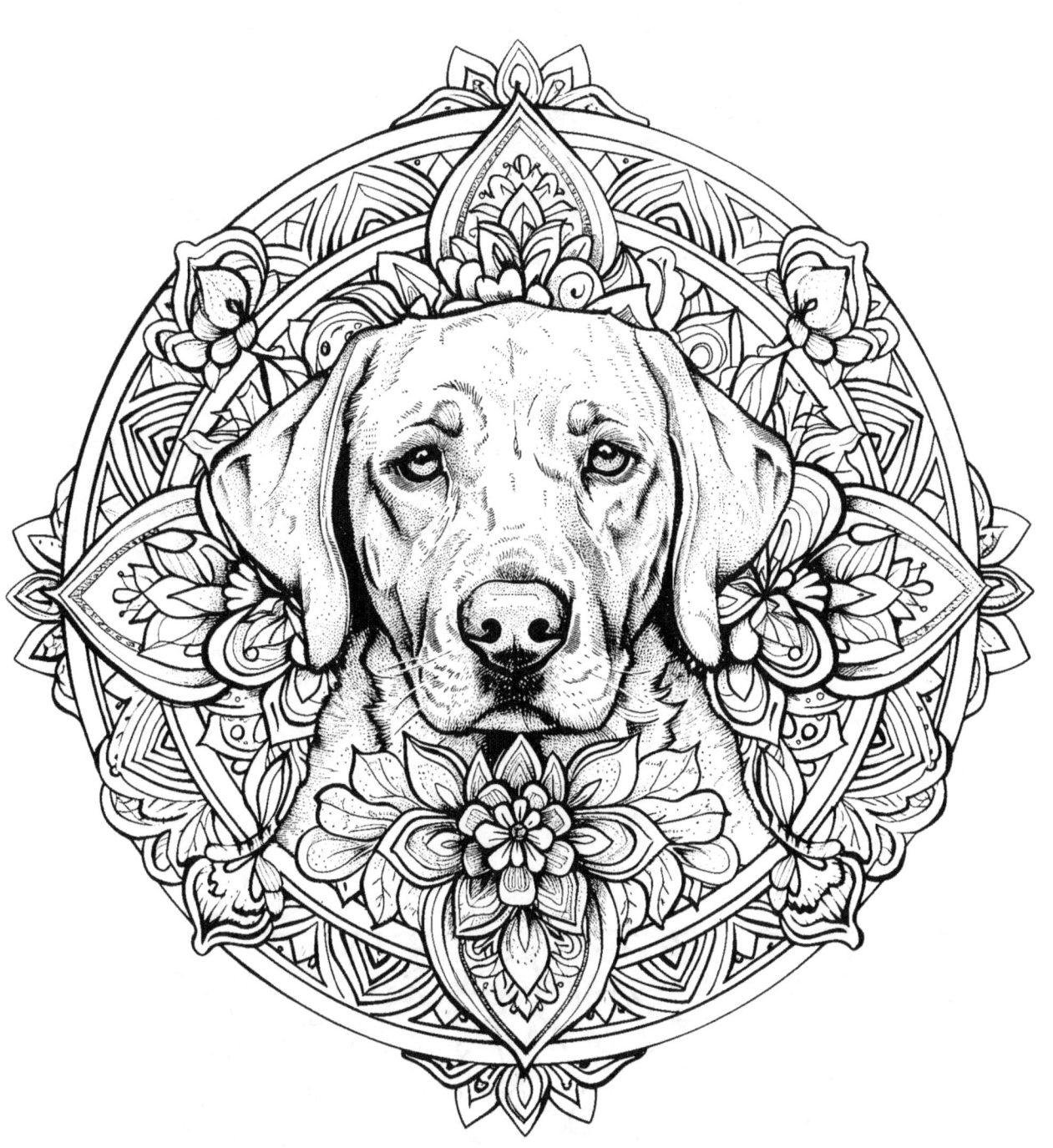

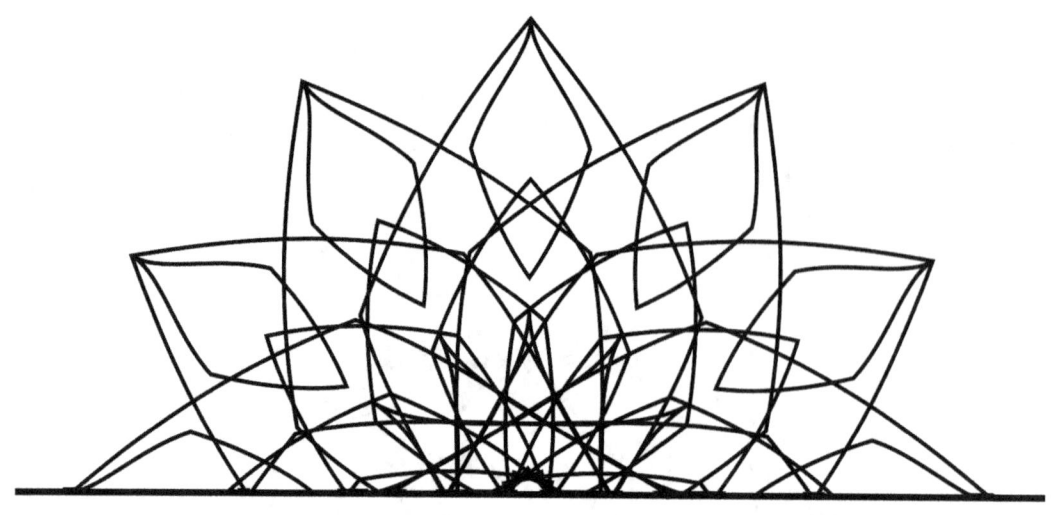

Labradors have excellent endurance and can run long distances.

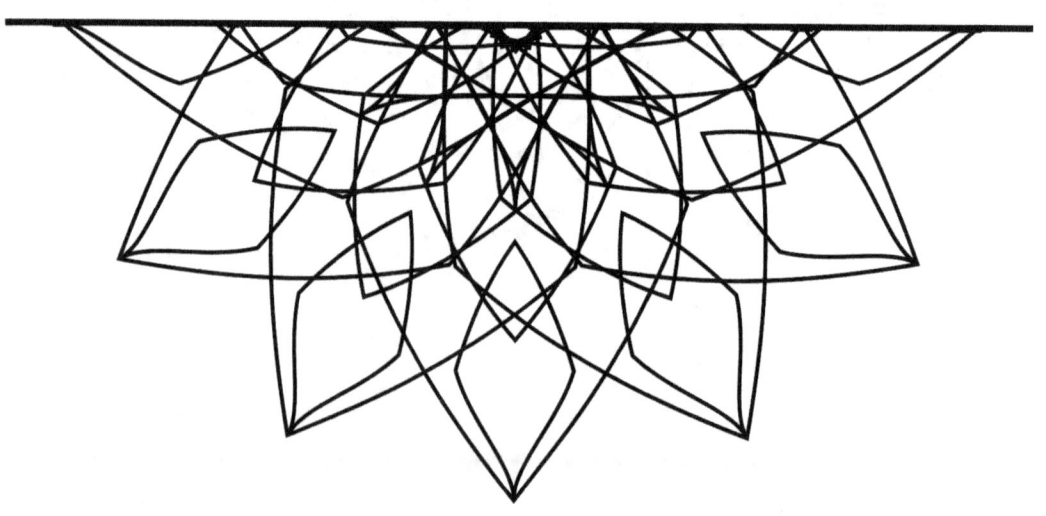

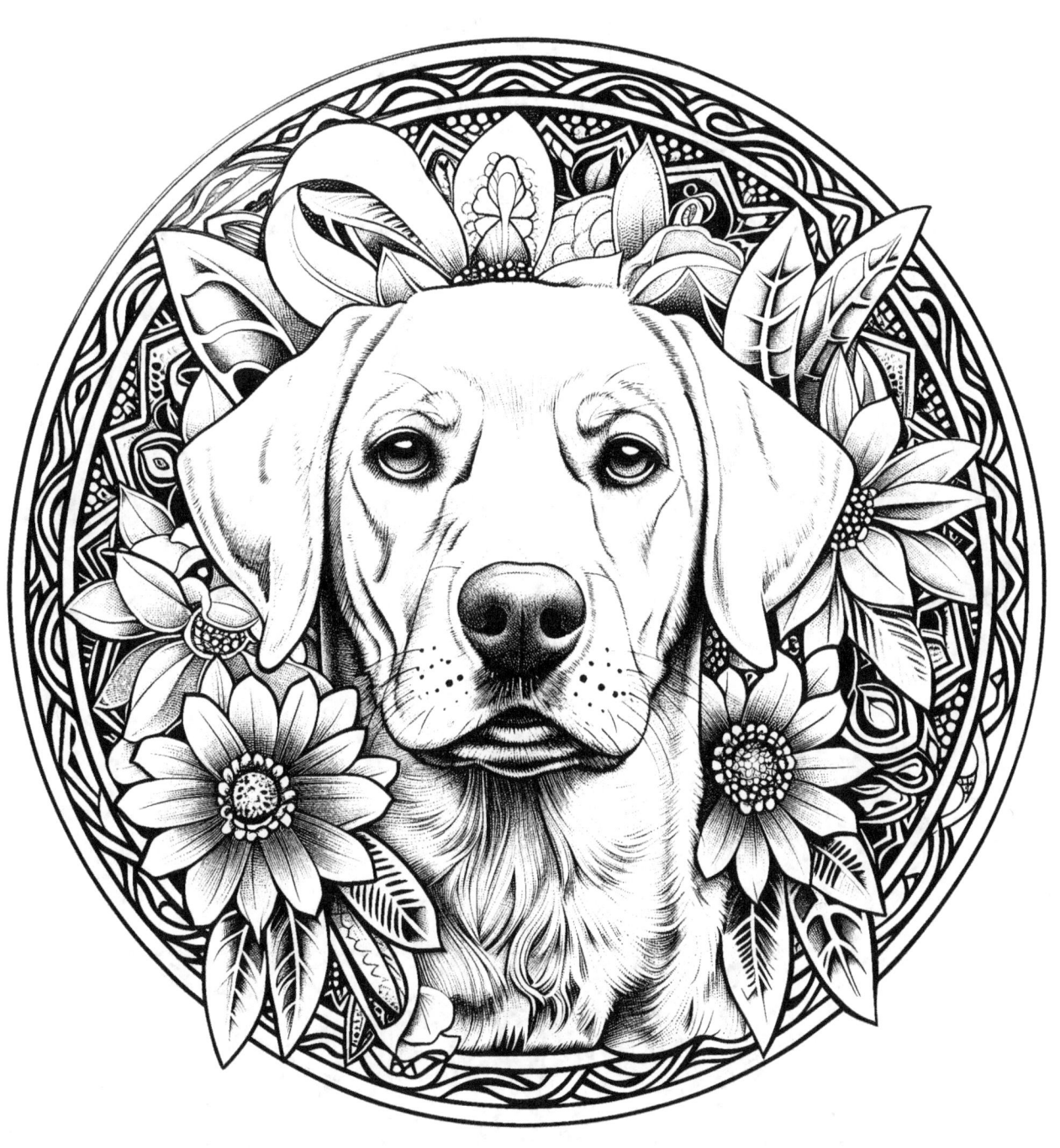

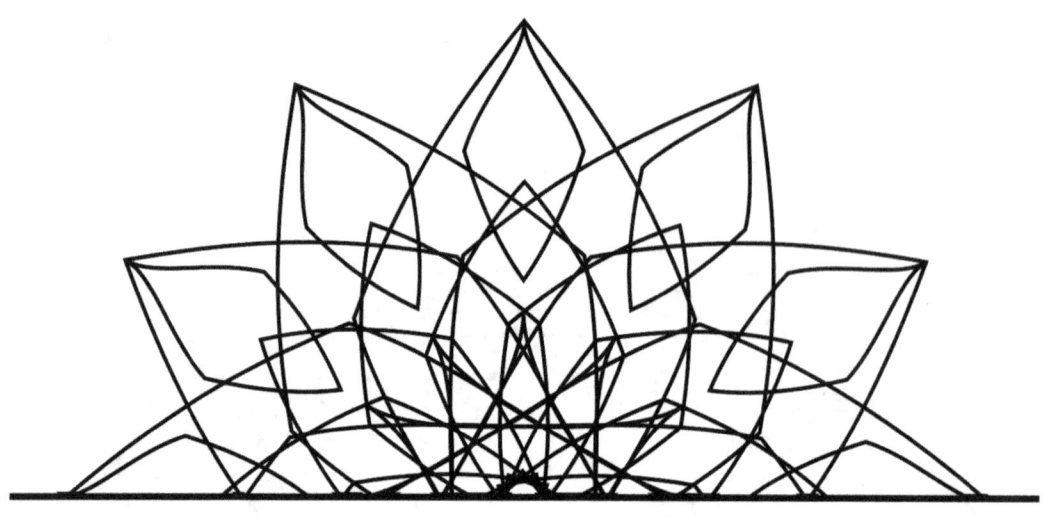

They are known for forming close bonds with children and serving as great playmates.

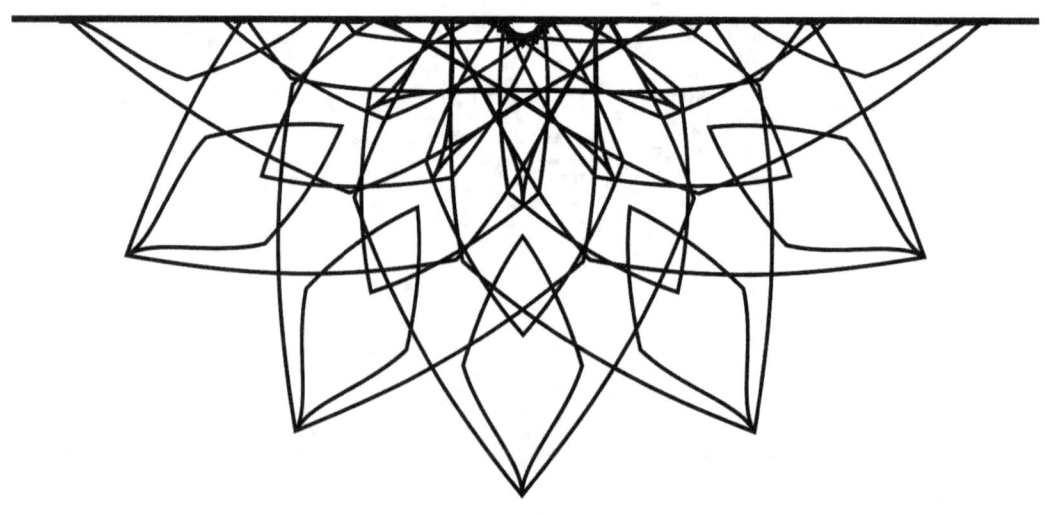

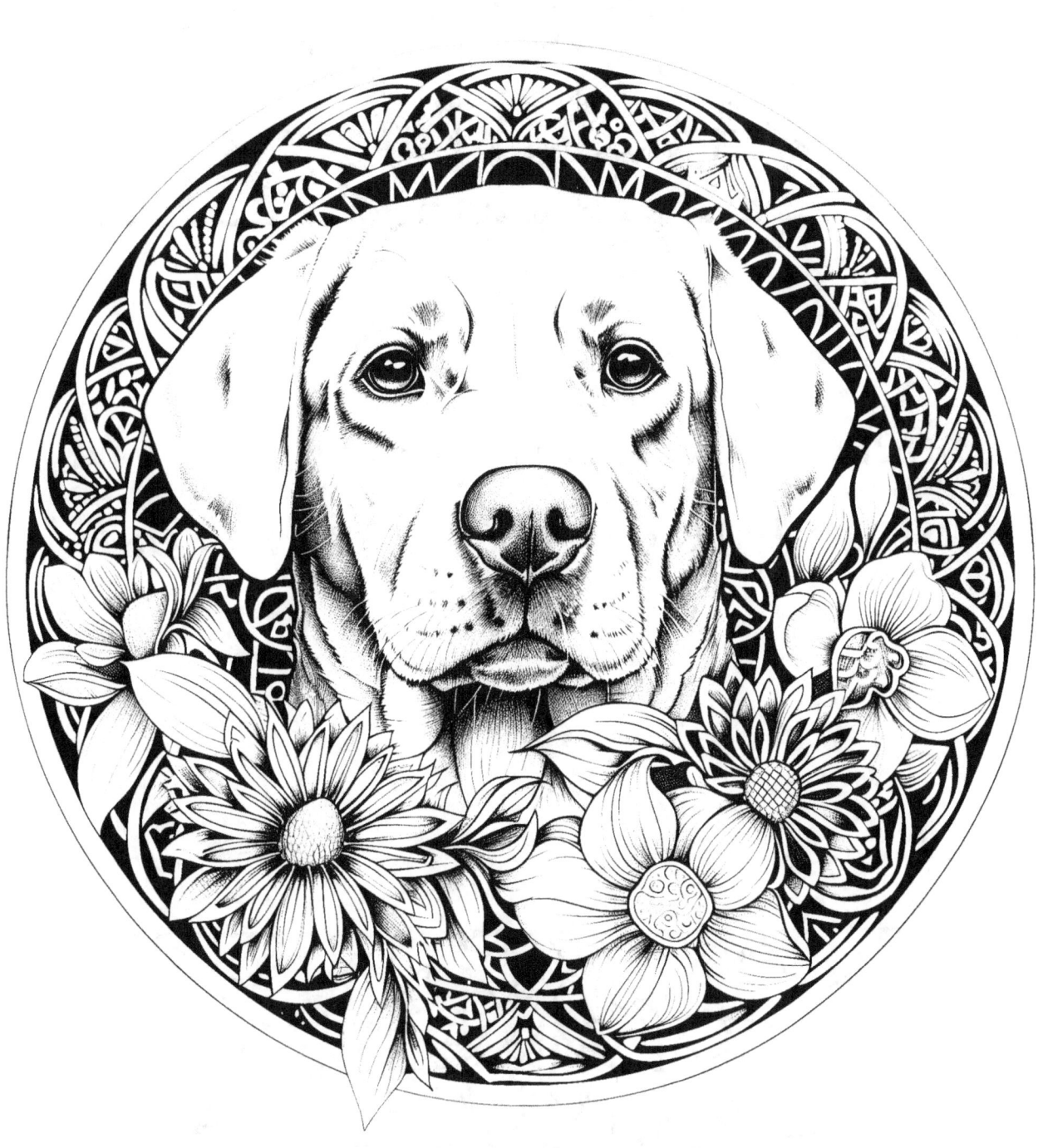

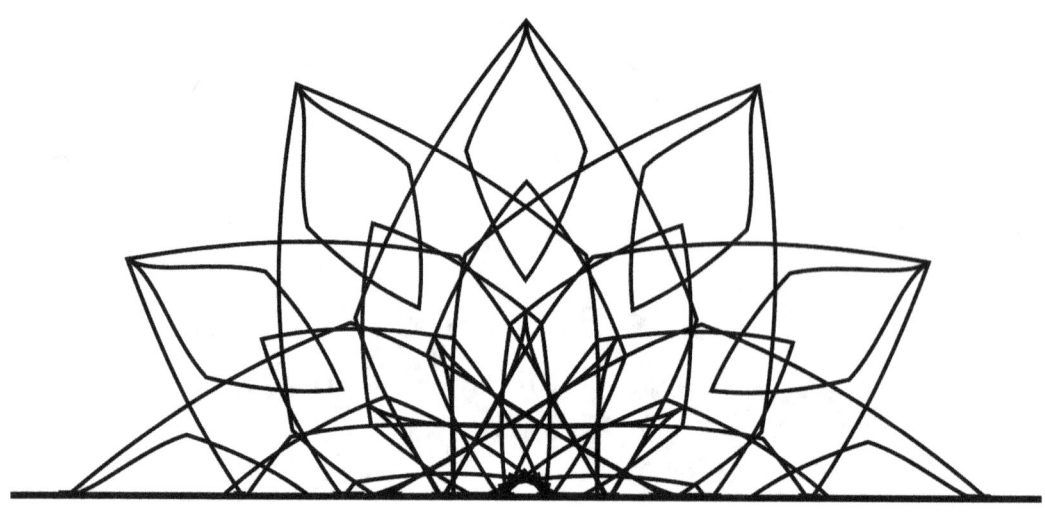

These dogs can make a variety of sounds to express their needs.

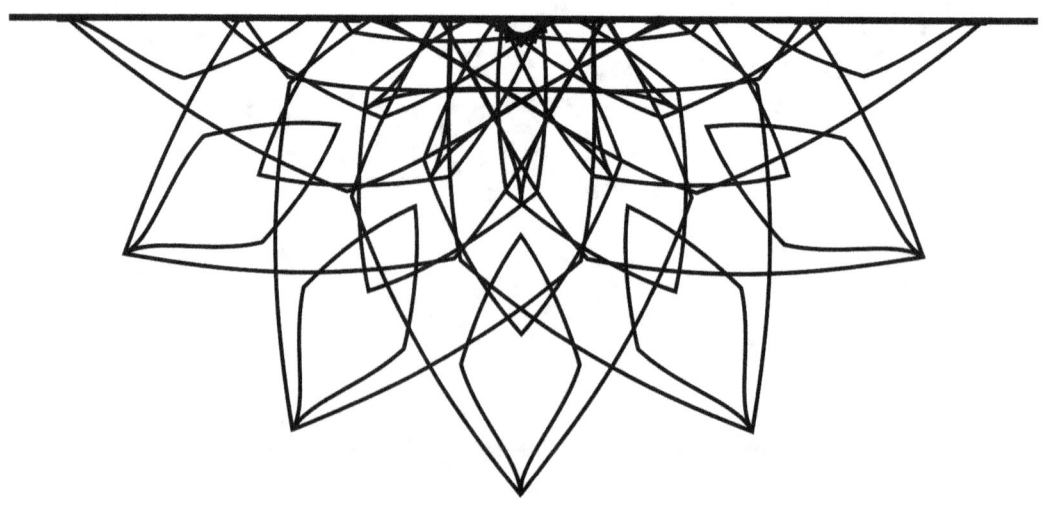

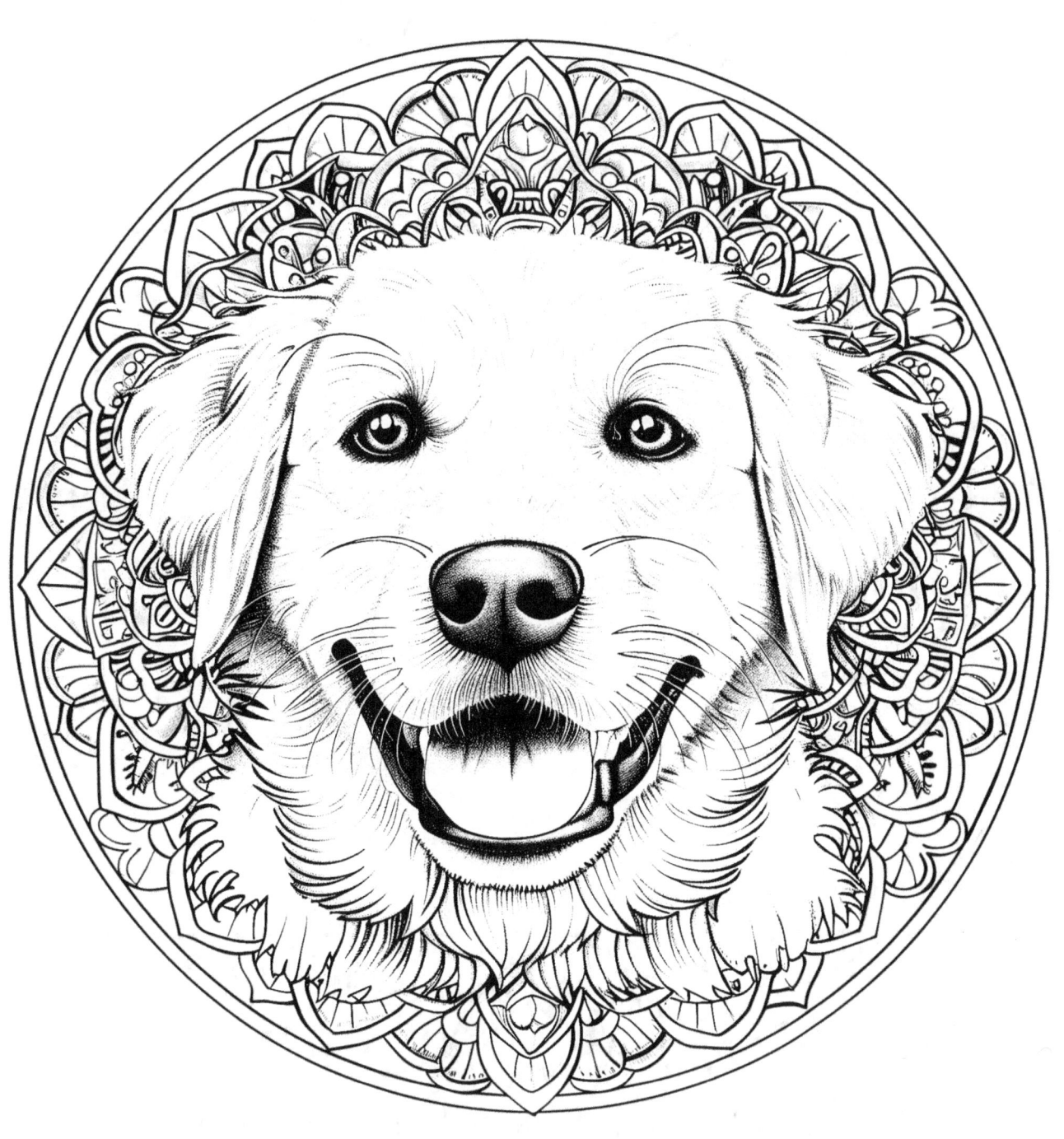

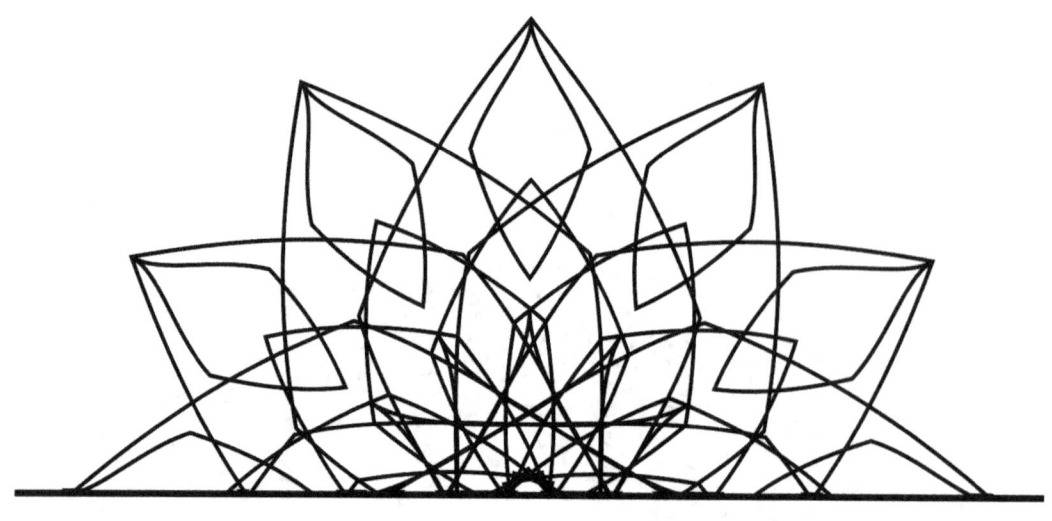

Labradors are very adaptable and can adapt well to different lifestyles.

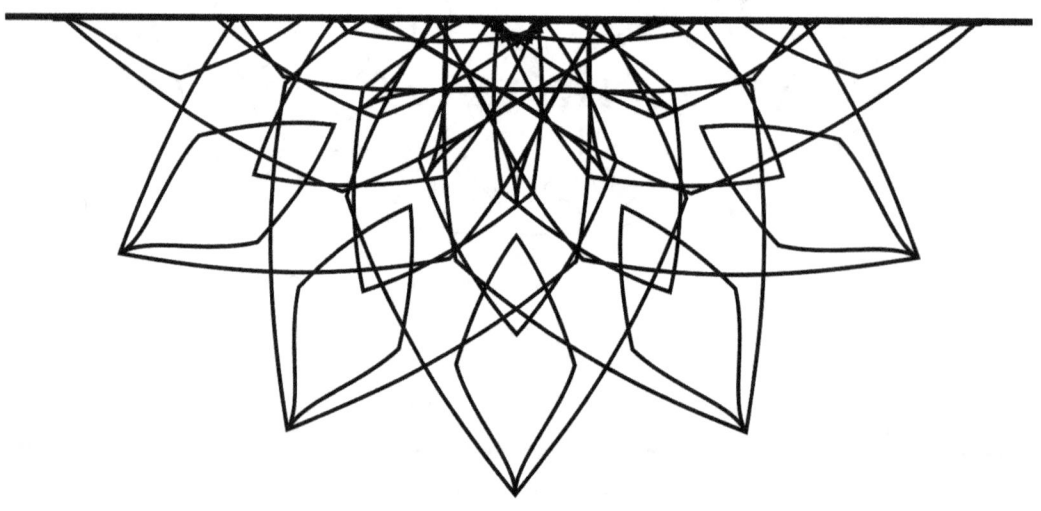

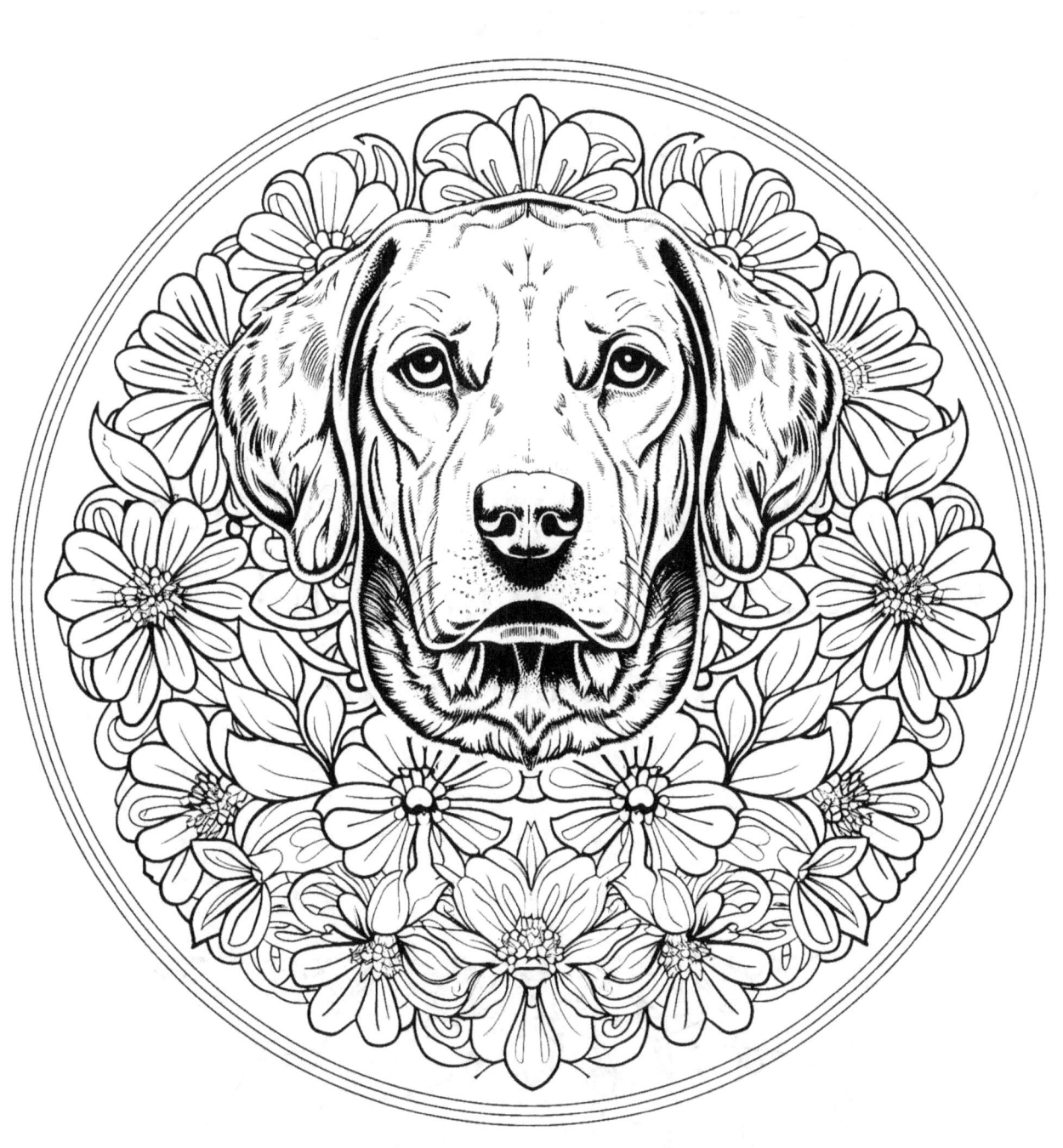

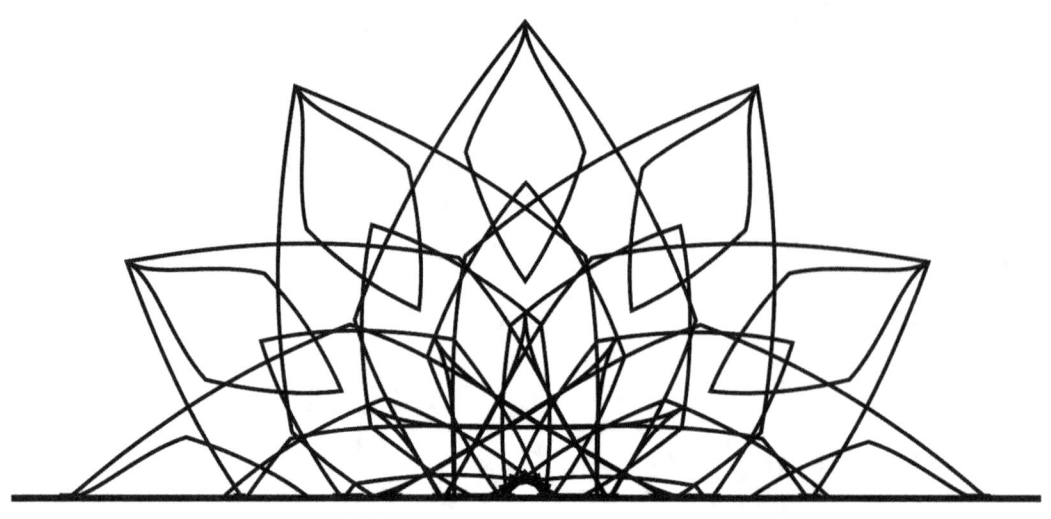

They have a natural inclination to make their owners happy and are often very affectionate.

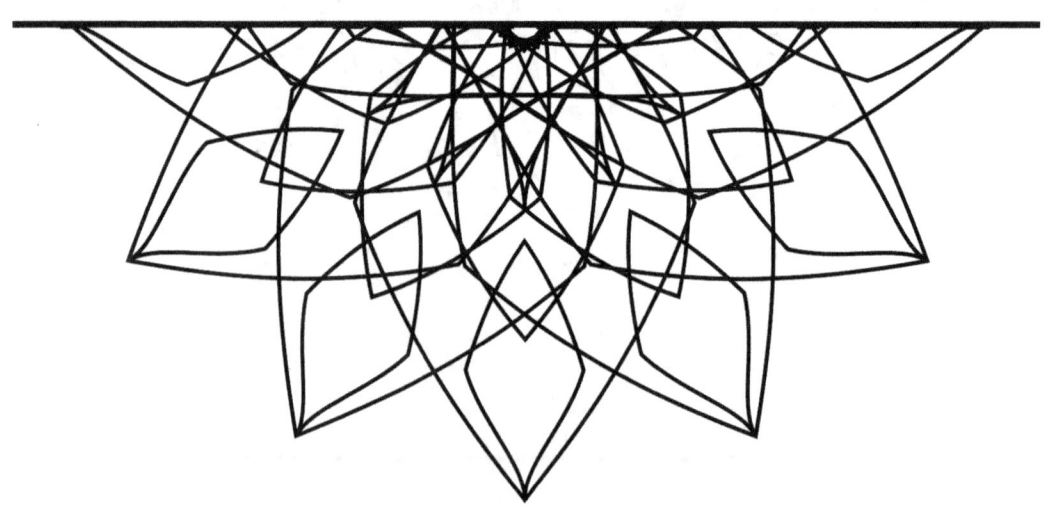

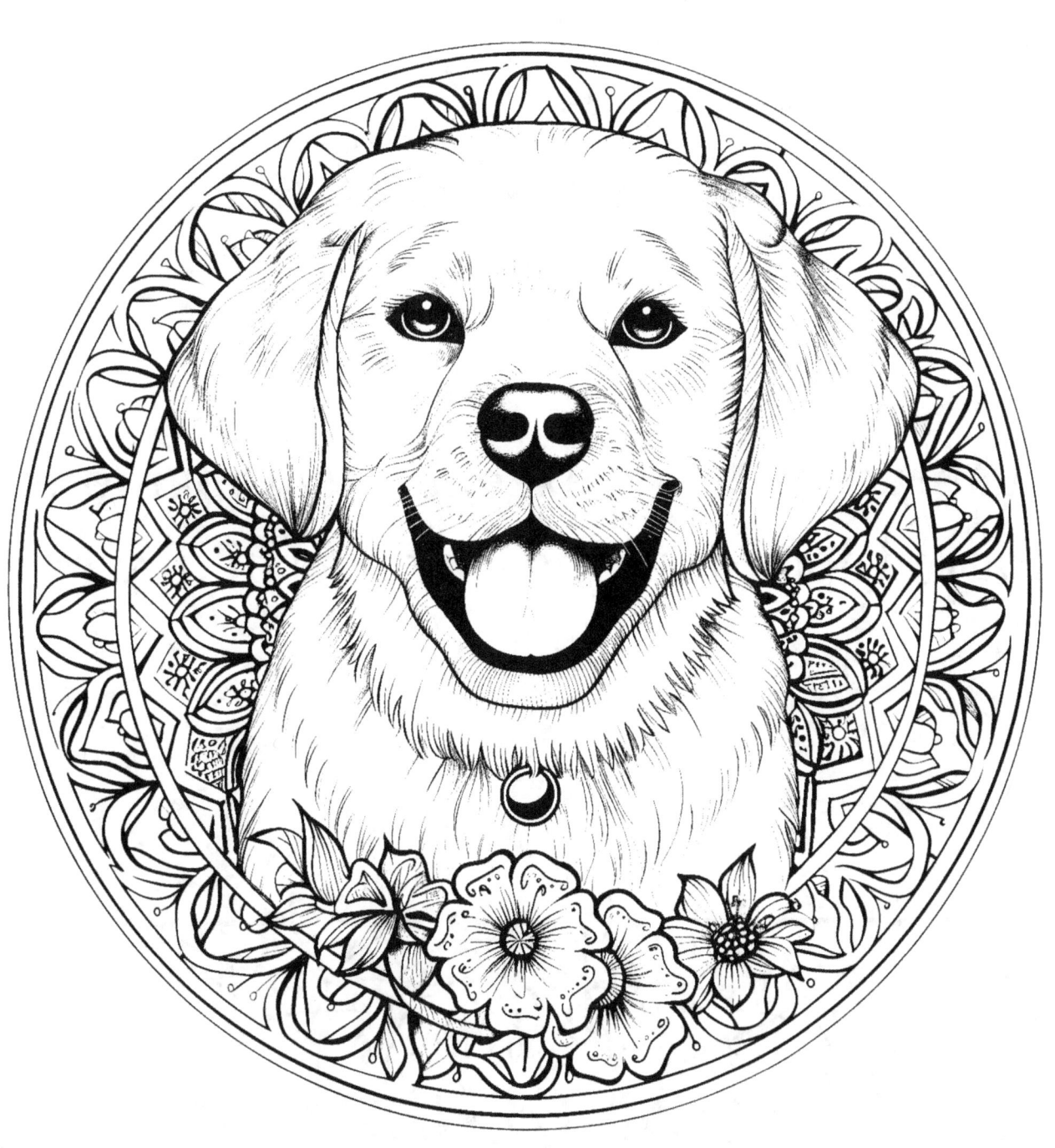

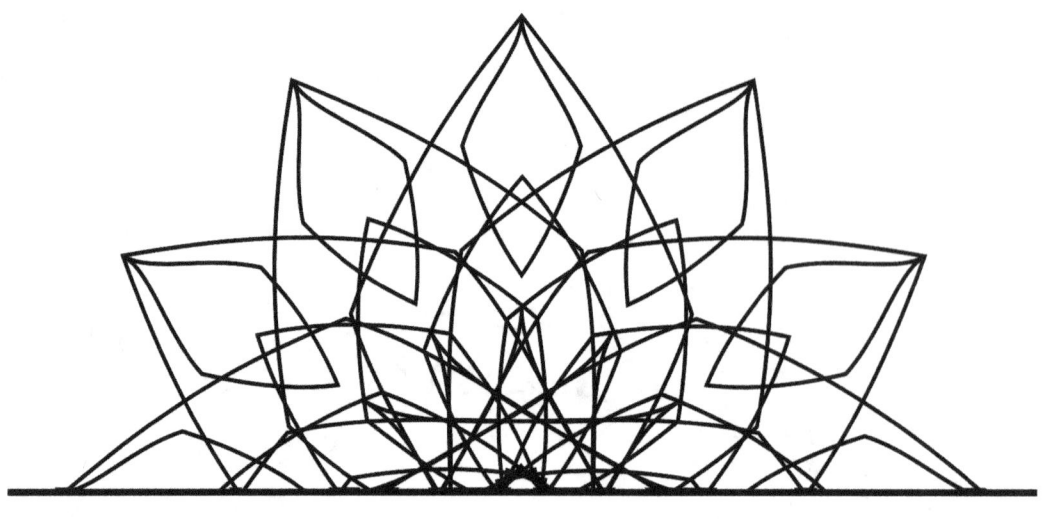

Labradors make excellent companions for outdoor activities such as hiking and jogging.

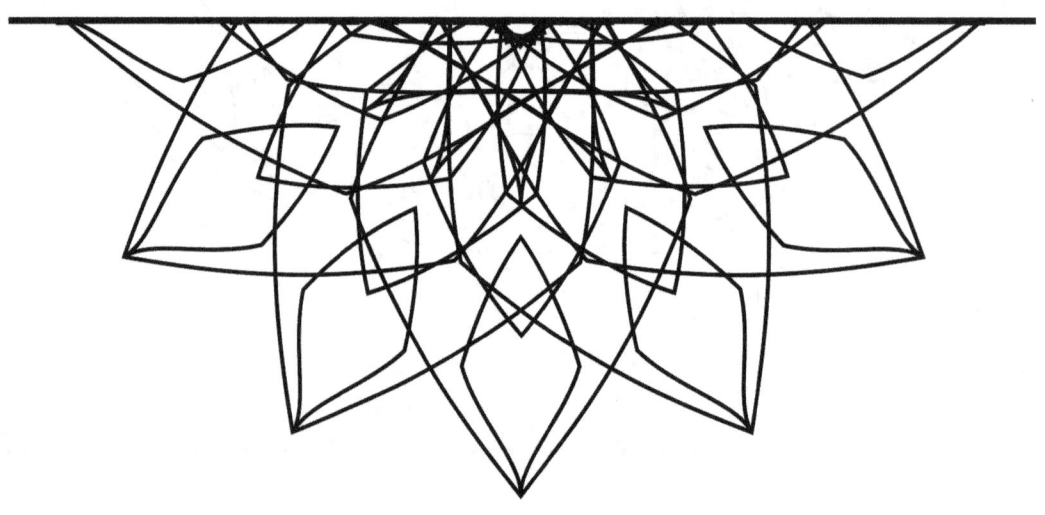

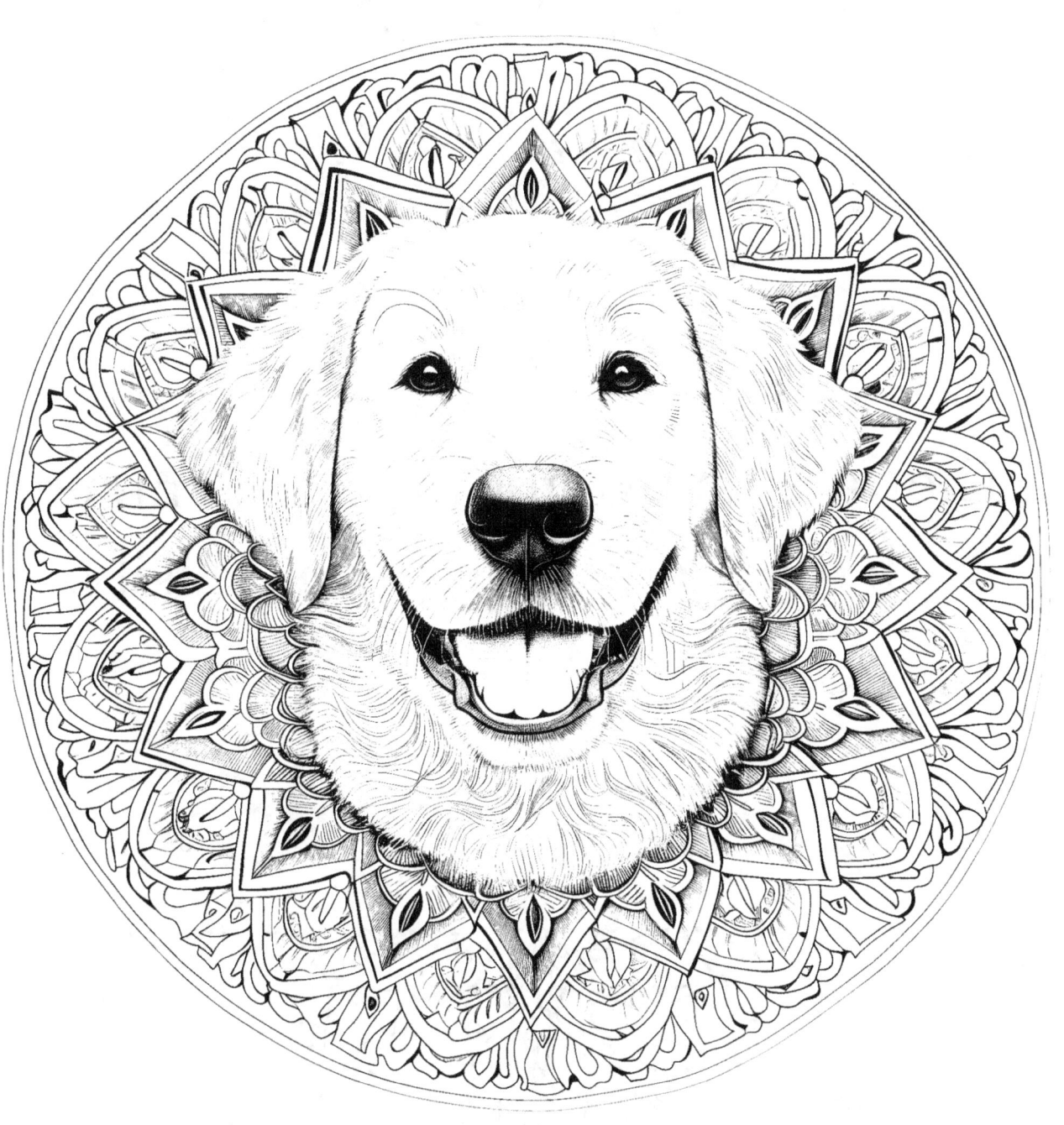

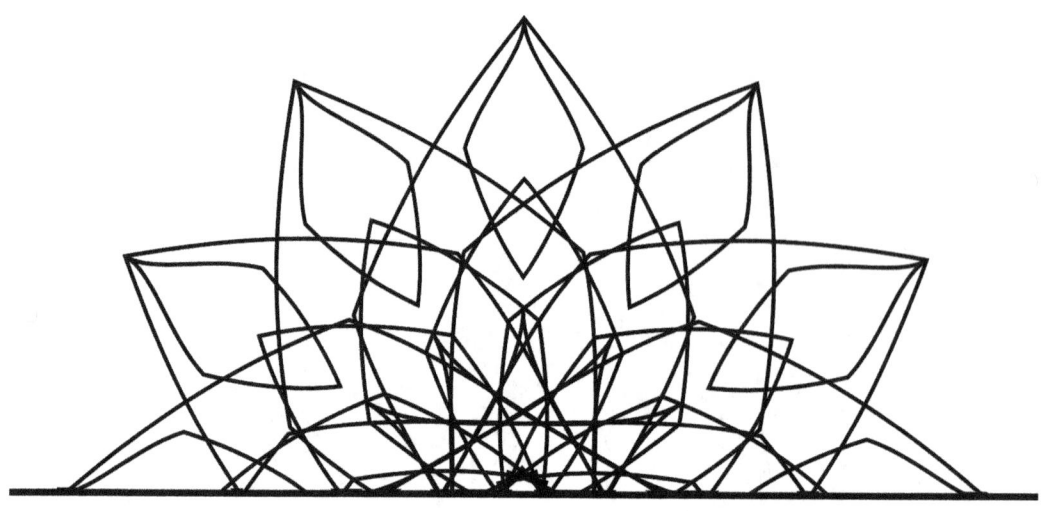

They are known for making contact with other dogs and people easily.

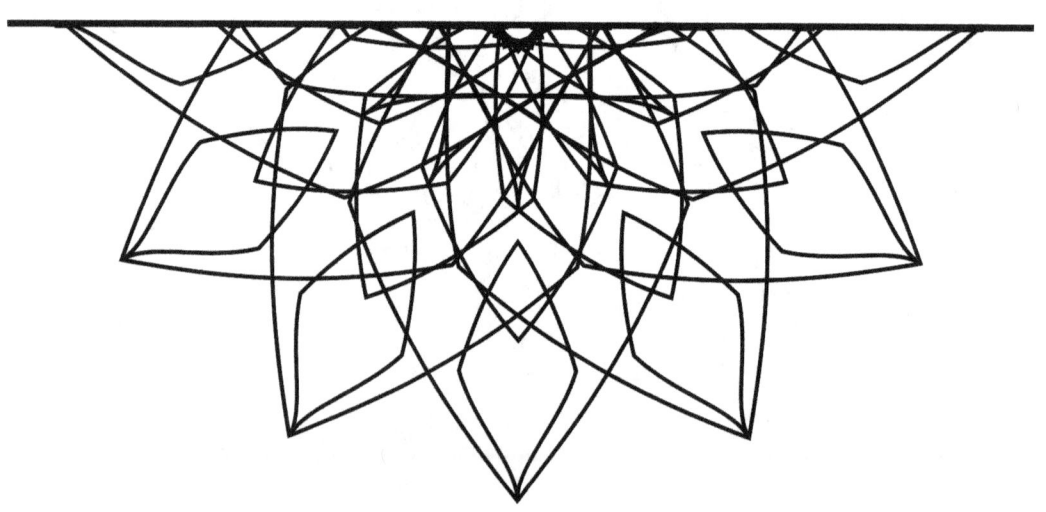

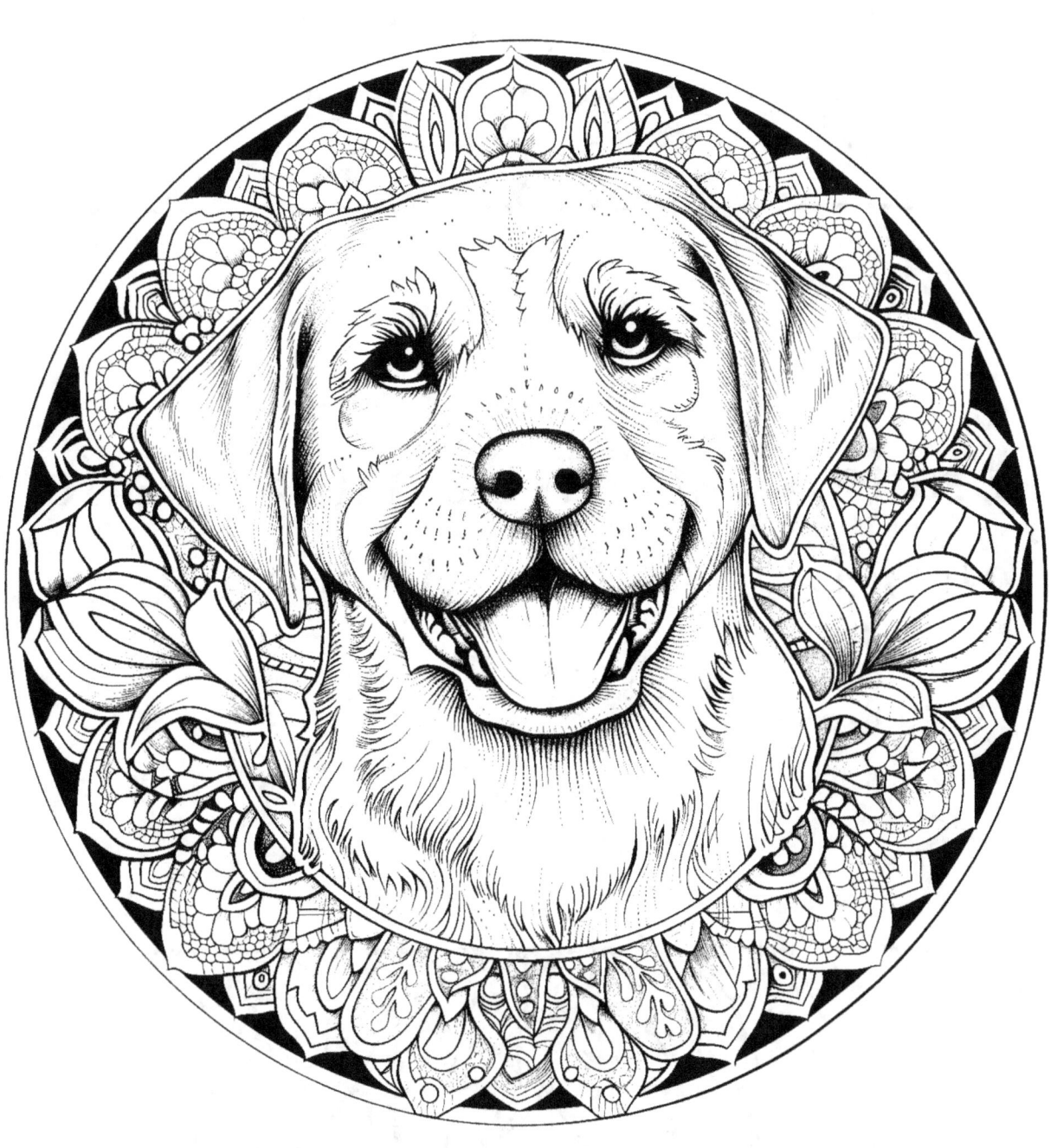

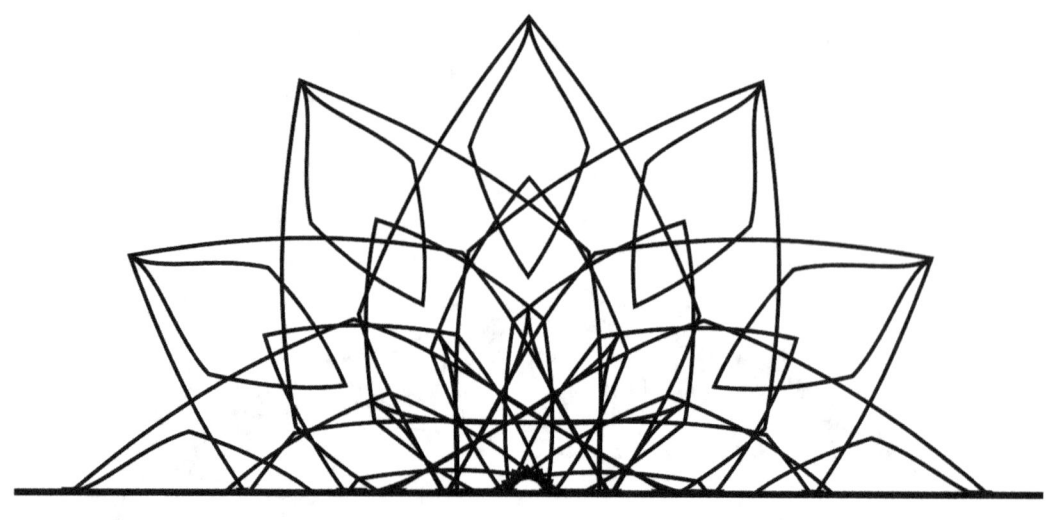

Labradors can have a calming effect on people and are often used as therapy dogs.

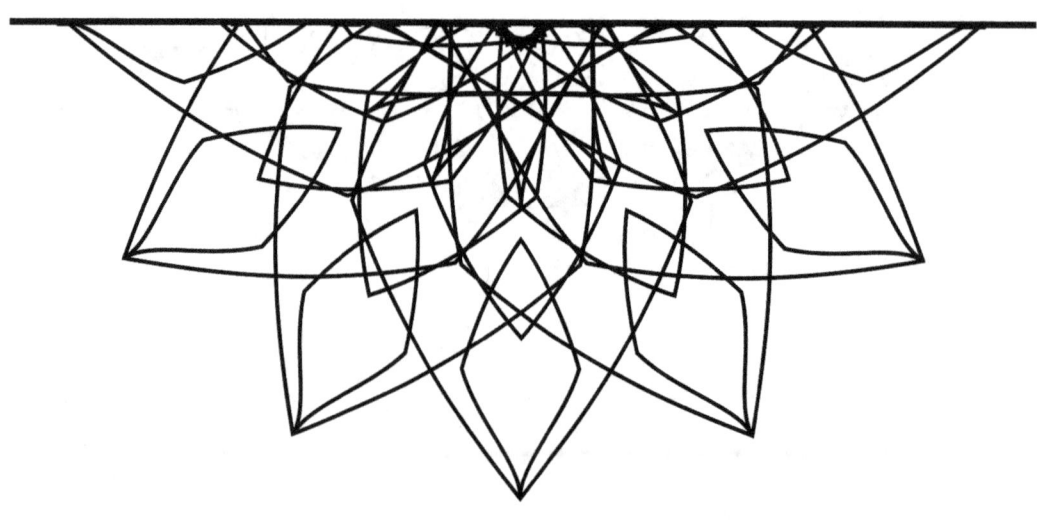

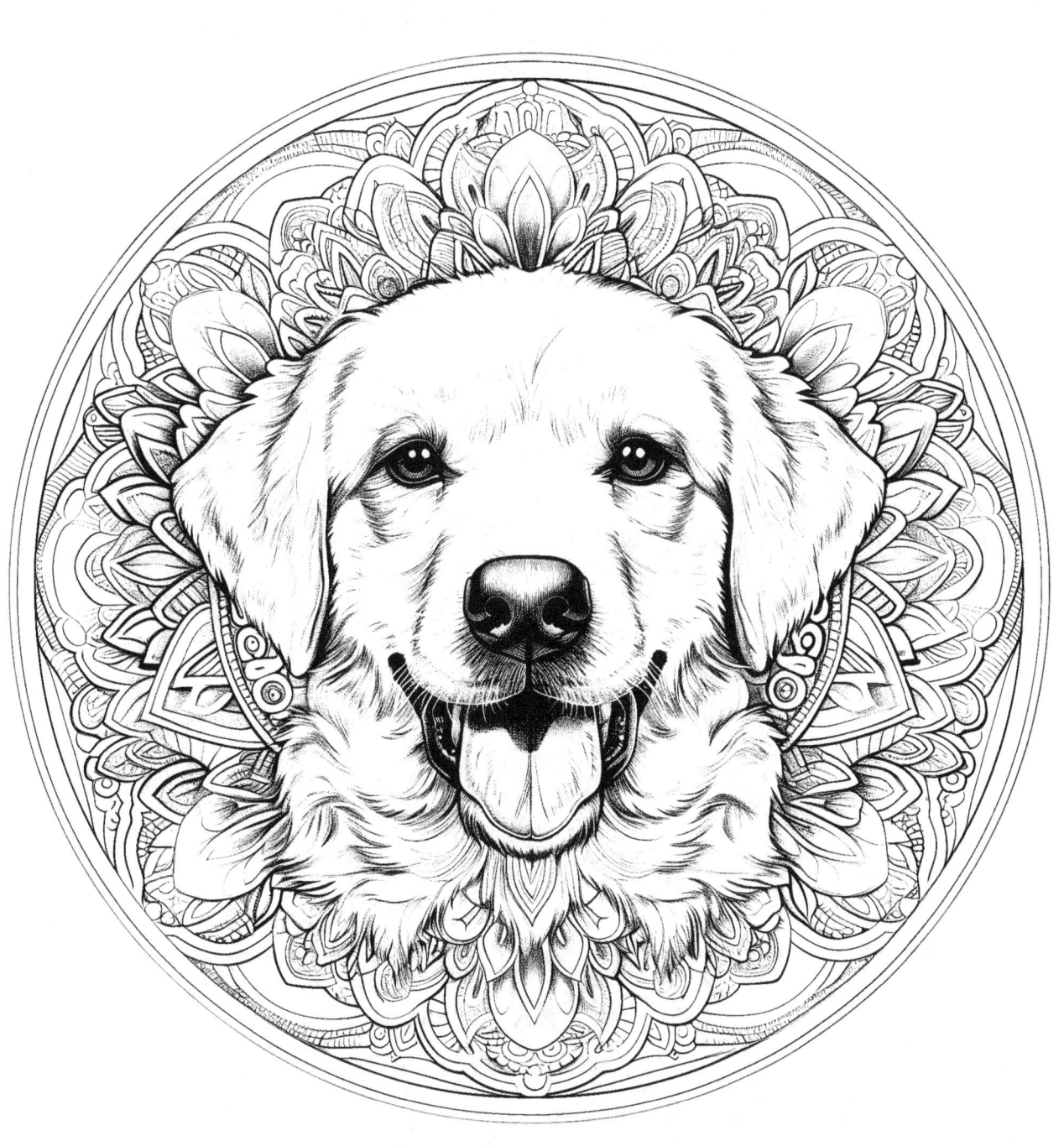

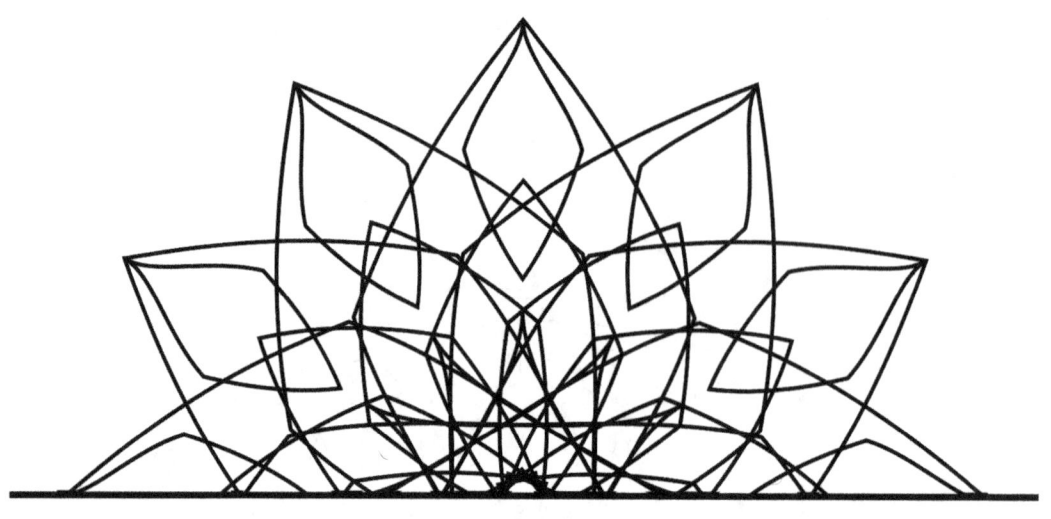

These dogs tend to follow their owners everywhere and are very loyal.

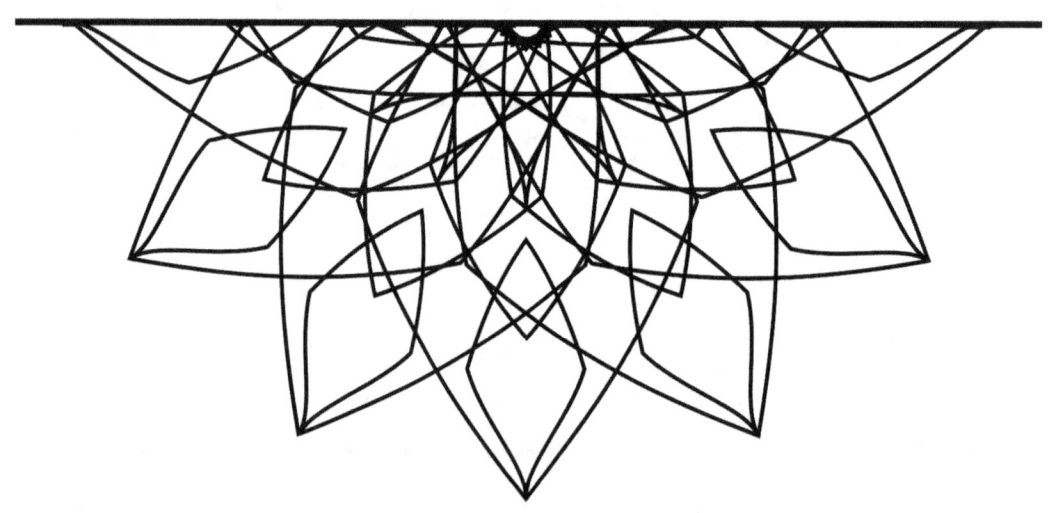

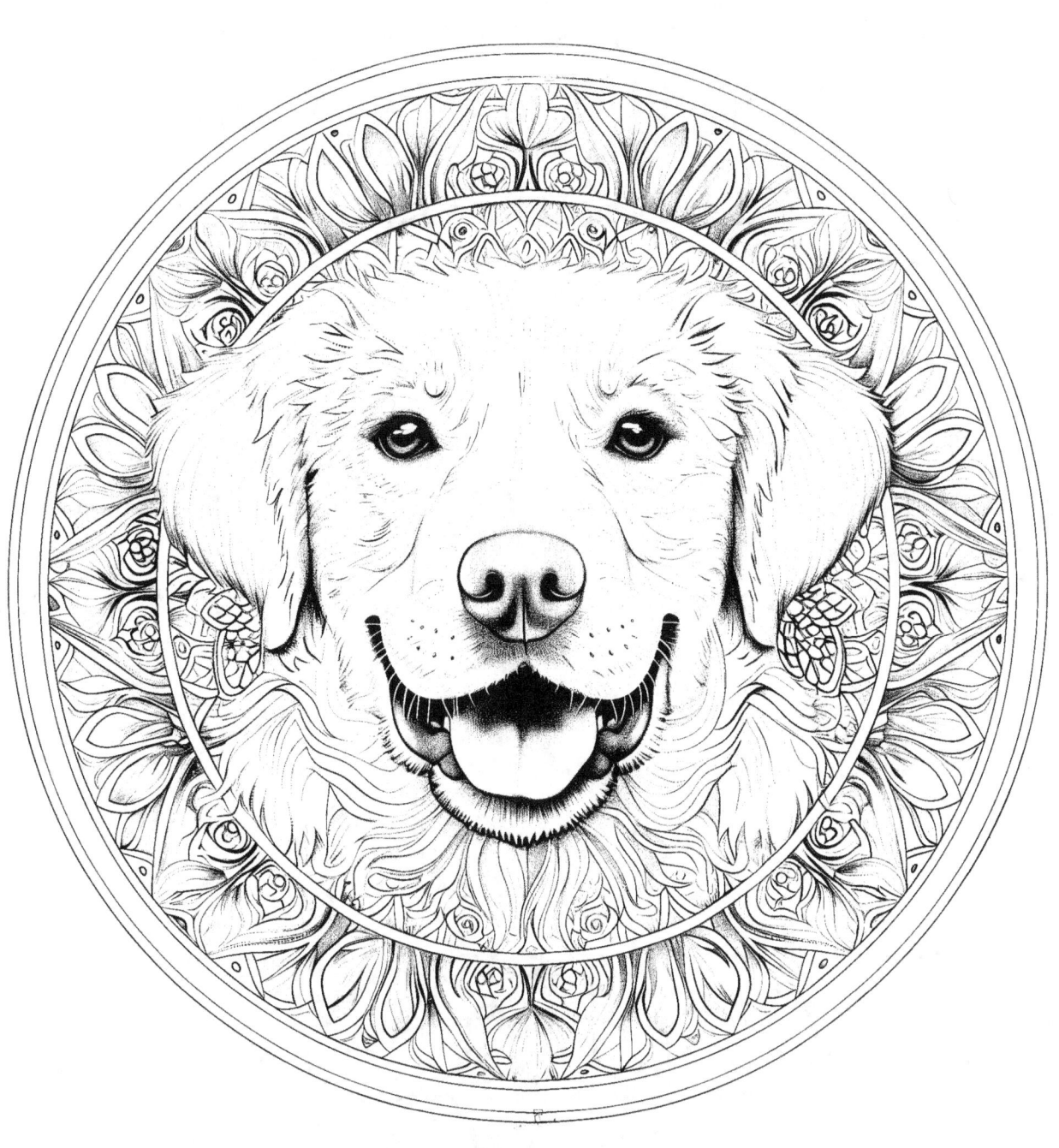

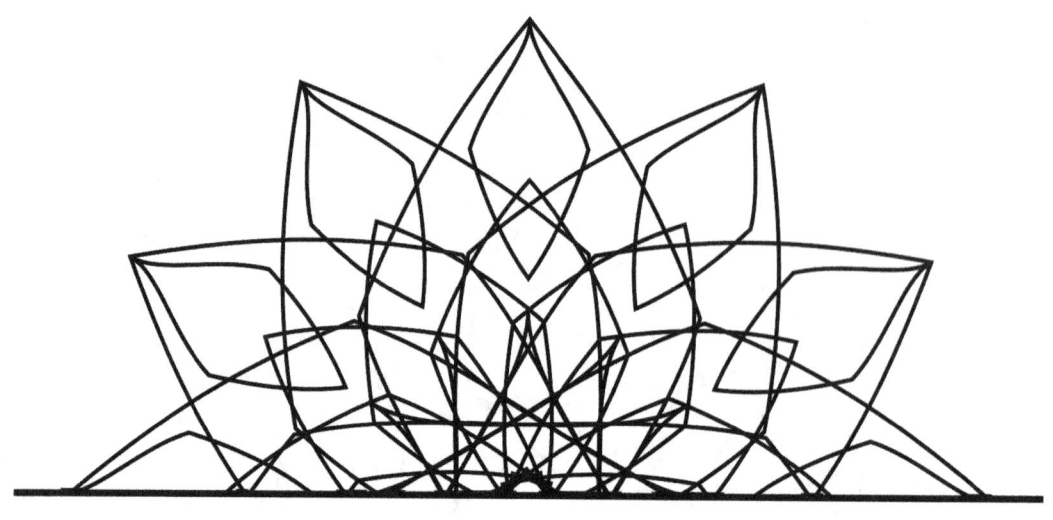

Labradors have strong bite force and can carry large prey while retrieving.

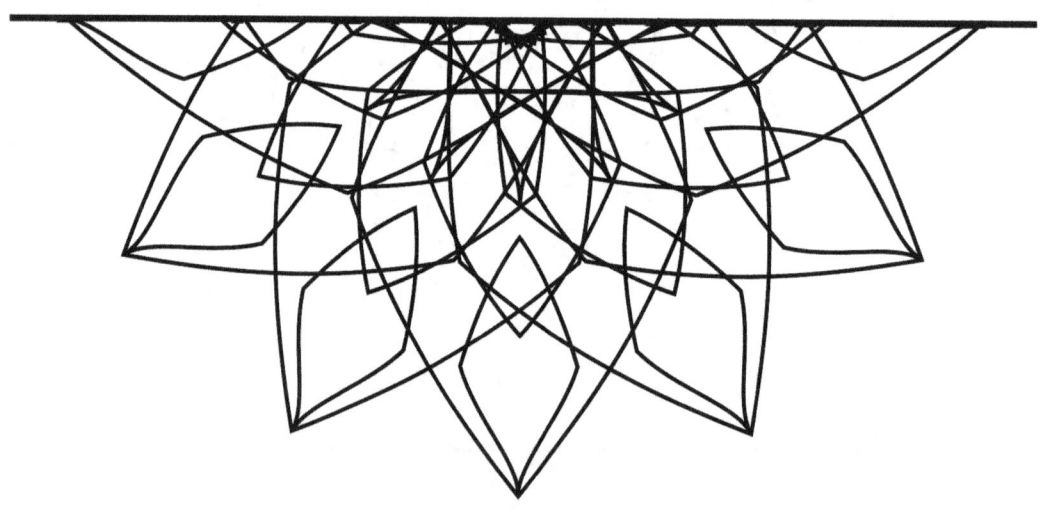

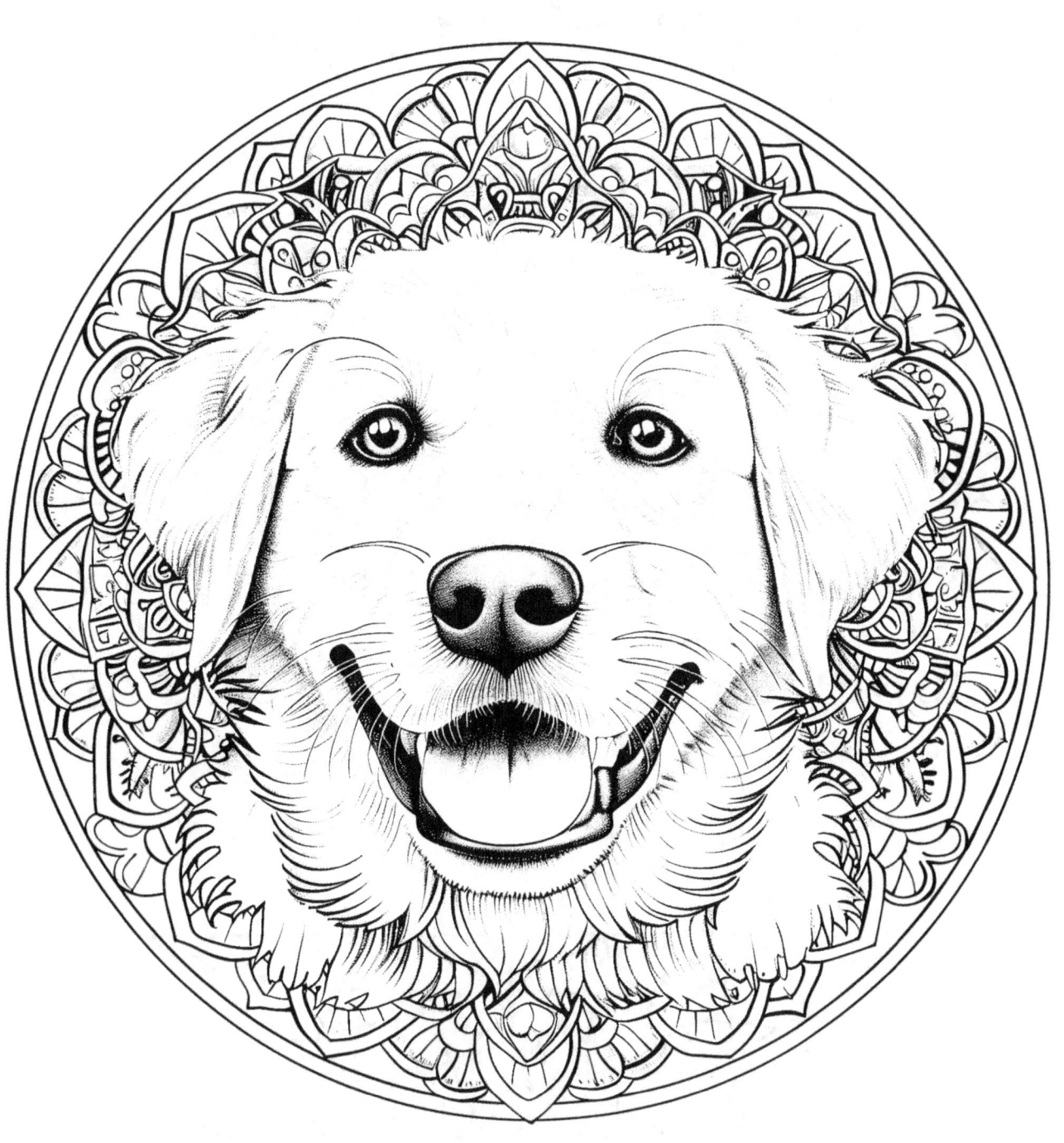

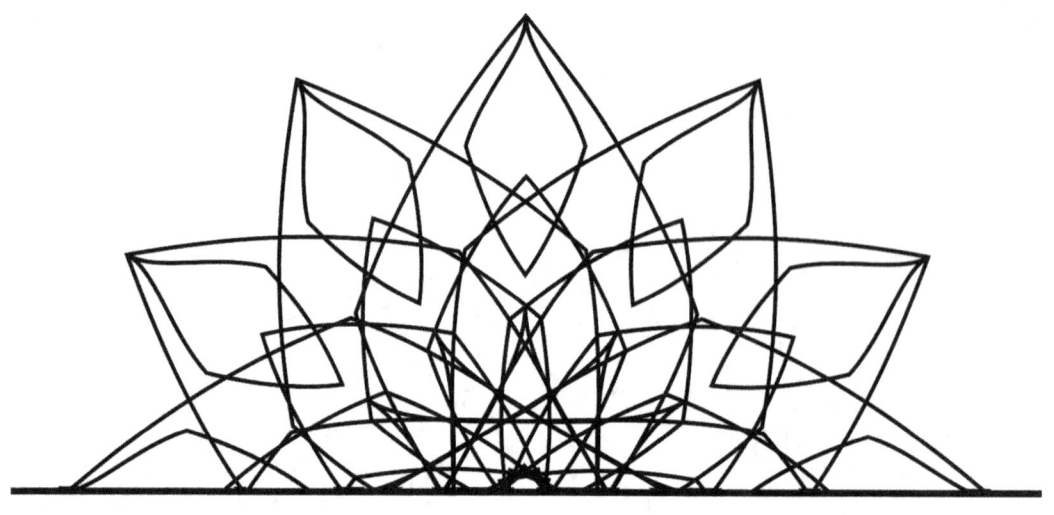

They are often involved in water rescue missions and can help people in emergency situations.

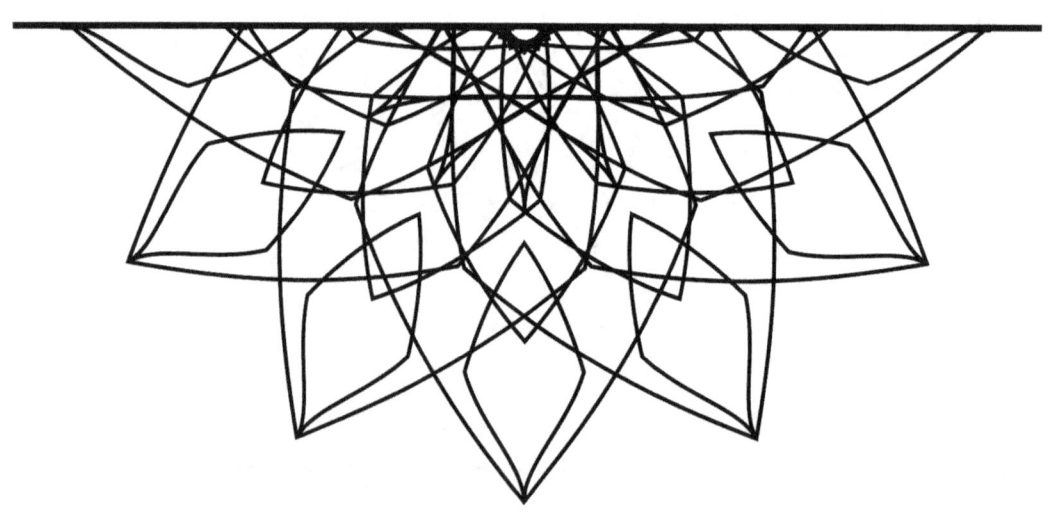

More enchanting creations

(product images exude the charm of a coloring book in black and white. Simply scan the QR code to unveil the vibrant color palette)

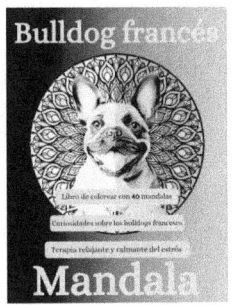 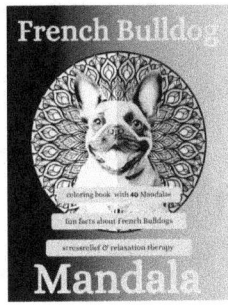 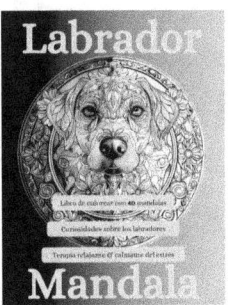 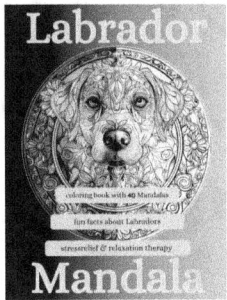

ASIN: B0D1KS2LMG   ASIN: B0D1N9N1LR   ASIN: B0D1GNZCPZ   ASIN: B0D1NFC6M7

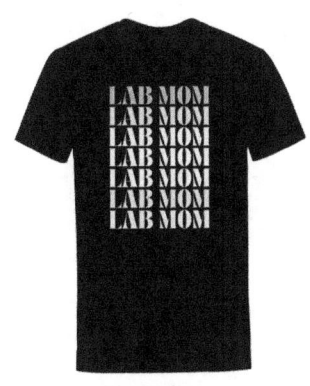 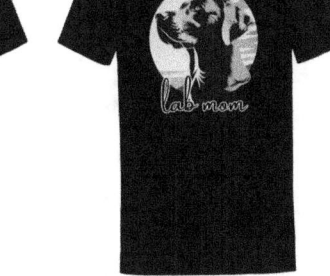 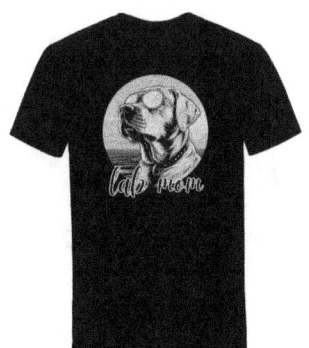 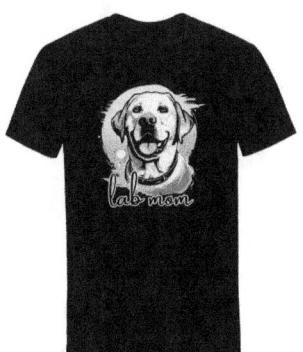

Imprint:

© 2024 StrassBook

Embodied by Stefan Strassburg

Berlin

paperback
ISBN: 979-8322321637.

If our product has brought you joy, kindly share your feedback.

www.ingramcontent.com/pod-product-compliance
Lightning Source LLC
Chambersburg PA
CBHW062117220526
45471CB00010B/3776